Safeguarding Future Intelligence: Data Protection and Security Strategies in the age of AI

Anil Kumar Yadav Yanamala

Table of contents

Chapter 1: Understanding the Human Element in Cybersecurity

Chapter 2: Building a Security-Aware Culture

Chapter 3: Training and Education for Cybersecurity Awareness

Chapter 4: Risk Management and Mitigation Strategies

Chapter 5: Future Trends and Evolving Challenges

Author Bio

Anil Kumar Yadav Yanamala achieved in the field of AI and data protection is a significant milestone, often marked by contributions to improving privacy, security, and ethical standards in the ever-evolving digital landscape. It involves the development of innovative solutions that safeguard personal data while balancing the need for technological advancement. Achieved in AI and data protection within government institutions which are crucial for ensuring the privacy and security of citizens' data while implementing advanced technologies. Governments worldwide are increasingly adopting AI to improve public services, cybersecurity, and data management. However, with this adoption comes the responsibility to protect sensitive information and uphold ethical standards.

Reviewers

Srikanth Suryadevara is a highly experienced Senior .NET Developer and Technical Lead with over 12 years of expertise in designing, developing, and maintaining robust applications and systems. Proficient in a wide range of .NET frameworks, C#, ASP.NET, angular and related Microsoft technologies, Srikanth Suryadevara has a proven track record of leading technical teams, architecting solutions, and driving innovation in complex software projects. With a deep understanding of software development life cycles, he excels in delivering scalable, high-performance solutions that meet both technical and business requirements.

Chapter 1: Understanding the Human Element in Cybersecurity

1.1 Introduction to Human Factors in Cybersecurity
1.2 The Role of Human Behavior in Security Risks
1.3 Common Security Mistakes and Their Impact
1.4 Case Studies: Human Error in Major Cyber Incidents
1.5 Summary and Key Takeaways

Chapter 1: Understanding the Human Element in Cybersecurity

In the ever-evolving world of cybersecurity, the role of human behavior remains a critical factor in both strengthening and weakening security measures. This chapter delves into the significance of the human element in cybersecurity, focusing on how individuals within an organization—be they employees, customers, or external actors—can become both the first line of defense and the weakest link in the security chain. The chapter begins by exploring common human vulnerabilities such as poor password hygiene, susceptibility to phishing attacks, and the failure to recognize or report suspicious activity. Despite advanced technologies, human error continues to be one of the primary causes of data breaches and security incidents. This section highlights real-world examples of cyberattacks that were enabled by human lapses, demonstrating the high stakes of cybersecurity.

Moreover, the chapter emphasizes the importance of cultivating a culture of cybersecurity awareness. It discusses the role of training programs, simulations, and continuous education in empowering individuals to recognize threats and take proactive steps to mitigate risks.

A well-informed workforce can serve as a powerful deterrent to cyber threats, but this requires consistent and up-to-date training initiatives.

Additionally, the chapter examines insider threats—both malicious and unintentional. While external hackers often garner more attention, insiders with privileged access to sensitive data can cause significant damage. The complexity of human motivations and the challenge of predicting behavior make insider threats particularly difficult to address, but proper access controls, monitoring, and behavioral analysis tools can help mitigate these risks.

In conclusion, understanding and managing the human element is crucial for building a robust cybersecurity strategy. This chapter lays the foundation for how addressing human factors, through education and security policies, plays a pivotal role in defending against cyber threats.

Introduction

In the realm of cybersecurity, the technological and procedural aspects often dominate discussions, overshadowing a critical factor: the human element. Despite advancements in security technology, the majority of security breaches and incidents are attributed to human behavior. Understanding this human element is essential for developing effective strategies to mitigate risks and enhance organizational security. Human behavior plays a pivotal role in cybersecurity, influencing both the likelihood of security incidents and the effectiveness of security measures. Employees' actions, whether intentional or accidental, can significantly impact the security posture of an organization. From falling prey to phishing attacks to mishandling sensitive information, human errors and lapses in judgment are frequent catalysts for security breaches.

Common Security Mistakes and Their Impact

Common security mistakes include weak password practices, failure to update software, neglecting security training, and insufficient awareness of phishing tactics. These behaviors create vulnerabilities that can be exploited by malicious actors. For instance, weak passwords can be easily cracked, while outdated software may harbor unpatched vulnerabilities. The consequences of these mistakes can be severe, ranging from financial loss to reputational damage and legal repercussions. Analyzing case studies of major cyber incidents reveals how human errors have led to significant security breaches. For example, the 2017 Equifax data breach was largely attributed to an unpatched vulnerability and a failure to address known security issues promptly. Similarly, the 2014 Sony Pictures hack involved spear-phishing emails that targeted employees, leading to a massive data breach and operational disruption. These incidents underscore the critical need to address human factors in cybersecurity strategies.

The Psychological and Organizational Aspects of Security Behavior

Understanding the psychological and organizational aspects that influence security behavior is crucial for designing effective interventions. Factors such as risk perception, cognitive biases, organizational culture, and incentives play a role in shaping employees' security practices. For example, employees may underestimate the risk of phishing attacks or be influenced by a lack of awareness and training. Addressing these factors involves not only educating employees but also fostering a culture that prioritizes security and encourages proactive behavior.

Summary and Key Takeaways

In conclusion, the human element in cybersecurity is a multifaceted issue that requires a comprehensive understanding of behavioral patterns, psychological influences, and organizational dynamics. Effective cybersecurity strategies must account for human behavior and incorporate measures to address common mistakes and foster a culture of security awareness. By recognizing the critical role of the human element, organizations can better manage security risks and enhance their overall security posture.

This introduction sets the stage for a deeper exploration of the human element in cybersecurity, highlighting its importance and the need for targeted strategies to address human-related risks.

1.1 Introduction to Human Factors in Cybersecurity

Human factors in cybersecurity refer to the complex interplay between people and the security systems designed to protect information and assets. Unlike purely technical aspects of cybersecurity, human factors focus on understanding how individuals' behaviors, perceptions, and decision-making processes influence security outcomes. The importance of human factors cannot be overstated, as human behavior often acts as both a source of vulnerability and a potential line of defense against cyber threats.

Understanding Human Behavior and Its Impact

Human behavior is a critical component of cybersecurity, with individuals often being the weakest link in the security chain. Employees, contractors, and even organizational leaders may inadvertently expose systems to risk through actions such as poor password management, falling for phishing schemes, or mishandling sensitive data. For instance, a study by Verizon in its 2020 Data Breach Investigations Report highlighted that social engineering attacks, which exploit human psychology, were responsible for a significant proportion of data breaches. This underscores the need to address human factors in cybersecurity strategies, as technological solutions alone cannot fully mitigate these risks.

Psychological Influences and Cognitive Biases

Psychological factors and cognitive biases play a significant role in how individuals interact with security measures. People often underestimate their susceptibility to cyber threats due to cognitive biases such as optimism bias or normalcy bias. These biases lead individuals to believe that security incidents are unlikely to happen to them, resulting in lax security practices. Additionally, the phenomenon of "security fatigue" can occur when individuals become overwhelmed by the complexities of security protocols, leading to decreased adherence to best practices. Understanding these psychological influences is crucial for designing effective security awareness programs and interventions that resonate with users and encourage compliant behavior.

Organizational Culture and Its Role

Organizational culture significantly impacts how employees approach cybersecurity. A culture that prioritizes security can foster a proactive attitude towards safeguarding information, whereas a culture that neglects or undermines security practices can lead to increased vulnerability. Leadership plays a crucial role in shaping this culture by setting the tone for security practices and reinforcing the importance of cybersecurity through policies, training, and communication. For example, organizations that implement regular security training and actively promote security awareness tend to have more engaged and informed employees who are better equipped to recognize and respond to threats.

The Need for Comprehensive Approaches

Addressing human factors in cybersecurity requires a comprehensive approach that integrates technical solutions with behavioral insights. This involves not only implementing robust security technologies but also educating users about security risks, creating a supportive security culture, and addressing the psychological barriers that impede secure behavior. Effective strategies include regular security awareness training, simulated phishing exercises, and fostering an environment where employees feel comfortable reporting potential security issues without fear of retribution. In summary, human factors in cybersecurity encompass a wide range of behavioral, psychological, and organizational influences that impact security outcomes. By understanding and addressing these factors, organizations can enhance their overall security posture and reduce the risk of cyber threats. This chapter will further explore these aspects, providing a detailed examination of how human behavior affects cybersecurity and offering practical strategies for improving security awareness and compliance.

The Role of Human Behavior in Security Risks

Human behavior is a fundamental determinant of security risks in any organization, profoundly influencing both the effectiveness of security measures and the vulnerability to cyber threats. Unlike purely technical vulnerabilities, human factors involve the ways in which individuals interact with, and sometimes undermine, security protocols. The role of human behavior in security risks manifests through a variety of actions and inactions that can inadvertently create or amplify vulnerabilities within an organization's security infrastructure.

Human Errors and Security Breaches

Human errors are a leading cause of security breaches and incidents. These errors can range from simple mistakes, such as accidentally sending sensitive information to the wrong recipient, to more complex failures, such as misconfiguring security settings or ignoring software updates. For example, research from the Ponemon Institute's 2021 Cost of a Data Breach Report highlighted that human error was the root cause of approximately 23% of data breaches. These errors often result from a lack of awareness, inadequate training, or cognitive overload, which can lead employees to overlook critical security protocols. The ramifications of such errors can be severe, including unauthorized access to sensitive data, financial loss, and damage to organizational reputation.

Phishing and Social Engineering

Phishing and social engineering attacks exploit human psychology to gain unauthorized access to systems and data. These attacks manipulate individuals into divulging confidential information or performing actions that compromise security. Phishing schemes, for instance, often involve deceptive emails or messages that appear to come from legitimate sources, tricking recipients into clicking malicious links or entering their credentials on fraudulent websites. The success of these attacks largely depends on human susceptibility to deceit and the ability of attackers to exploit common psychological vulnerabilities, such as trust and fear. According to the 2022 Verizon Data Breach Investigations Report, social engineering accounted for nearly 30% of breaches, underscoring the significant impact of human behavior on security risks.

Cognitive Biases and Security Behavior

Cognitive biases—systematic patterns of deviation from norm or rationality in judgment—affect how individuals perceive and respond to security risks. Biases such as optimism bias, where individuals believe they are less likely to be targeted by attacks, and normalcy bias, where people assume that security threats are rare and not applicable to them, contribute to poor security practices. These biases can lead to a false sense of security, resulting in complacency towards security measures and protocols. For instance, employees may neglect to use strong, unique passwords or may disregard security warnings because they believe that cyber attacks are unlikely to happen to them. Addressing these biases requires tailored training and awareness programs that help individuals recognize and overcome these cognitive distortions.

Organizational Culture and Security Practices

The culture within an organization plays a critical role in shaping employee behavior regarding security. A culture that prioritizes security and actively promotes awareness can foster an environment where employees are more vigilant and proactive in adhering to security practices. Conversely, a culture that undervalues security or fails to provide adequate training can lead to increased vulnerability. Leadership and management have a significant influence on organizational culture, setting the tone for security practices through their actions, policies, and communication. Organizations that invest in creating a security-conscious culture through regular training, clear policies, and supportive environments often see improved compliance and reduced risk of security incidents. Human behavior is a central factor in security risks, affecting how individuals interact with security measures and respond to potential threats. Errors, biases, and organizational culture all play significant roles in shaping security outcomes. Addressing these factors involves understanding the underlying behaviors and implementing strategies that mitigate risks associated with human actions. By focusing on improving security awareness, addressing cognitive biases, and fostering a strong security culture, organizations can enhance their overall security posture and reduce the impact of human-related vulnerabilities.

Common Security Mistakes and Their Impact

In the landscape of cybersecurity, certain common mistakes frequently undermine the effectiveness of protective measures and lead to significant security breaches. These errors, often rooted in human behavior and organizational practices, can expose systems and data to various forms of cyber threats. Understanding these mistakes and their impacts is crucial for developing robust security strategies and mitigating risks effectively.

1. Weak Password Practices

One of the most prevalent security mistakes is the use of weak or easily guessable passwords. Despite the availability of guidelines for creating strong passwords, many users continue to use simple, repetitive, or easily guessable passwords, such as "password123" or "123456."

Weak passwords are particularly vulnerable to brute-force attacks, where attackers use automated tools to try numerous combinations until they gain access. According to a report by the Verizon Data Breach Investigations Report, compromised passwords were involved in approximately 80% of data breaches. The impact of weak passwords can be severe, leading to unauthorized access to sensitive accounts, data breaches, and potential financial losses. Organizations must enforce strong password policies, implement multi-factor authentication (MFA), and educate users about the importance of using complex and unique passwords for each account.

2. Inadequate Software Updates and Patching

Failure to regularly update and patch software is another common security mistake. Software updates and patches are essential for addressing vulnerabilities and fixing security flaws that could be exploited by attackers. Many breaches have occurred because systems were running outdated software with known vulnerabilities. For instance, the WannaCry ransomware attack in 2017 exploited a vulnerability in older versions of Microsoft Windows that had been patched in a later update. The impact of failing to apply updates includes increased susceptibility to malware infections, unauthorized access, and data breaches.

Organizations should implement a robust patch management process to ensure that all software and systems are up-to-date and protected against known threats.

3. Neglecting Security Training and Awareness

Another critical security mistake is neglecting to provide comprehensive security training and awareness programs for employees. Without proper training, employees may not recognize phishing attempts, social engineering scams, or other malicious activities. For example, a well-designed phishing email might trick an employee into revealing login credentials or downloading malware. The impact of insufficient training is often evident in increased susceptibility to attacks and poor adherence to security policies. Organizations should invest in regular, interactive security training sessions, conduct simulated phishing exercises, and provide resources to keep employees informed about emerging threats and best practices.

4. Poor Data Handling and Storage Practices

Improper handling and storage of sensitive data is a significant security mistake that can lead to data breaches and compliance issues. Common issues include storing sensitive data in unencrypted formats, failing to secure backups, and improper disposal of obsolete devices. For instance, sensitive information such as personal identification numbers or financial data stored in plaintext can be easily accessed by unauthorized individuals if compromised. The impact of poor data handling includes potential data breaches, legal consequences, and damage to organizational reputation. Organizations should adopt data encryption, ensure secure backup practices, and implement policies for the proper disposal of sensitive information to mitigate these risks.

5. Insecure Network Configurations

Insecure network configurations, such as misconfigured firewalls, exposed ports, and weak network segmentation, can leave an organization vulnerable to cyber attacks. For example, improperly configured firewall rules might allow unauthorized access to critical systems or services. The impact of these mistakes can be severe, resulting in unauthorized access, data breaches, and service disruptions. Organizations should perform regular network security assessments, implement strong network segmentation practices, and ensure that firewalls and other network defenses are properly configured and maintained.

6. Lack of Incident Response Planning

Failing to develop and implement an effective incident response plan is a critical oversight that can exacerbate the impact of security incidents. Without a clear plan, organizations may struggle to respond to and recover from breaches, leading to prolonged exposure, greater damage, and higher recovery costs. The absence of a structured response plan can also lead to confusion and inefficiency during a security incident. Organizations should establish a comprehensive incident response plan that includes clear procedures for detecting, containing, and mitigating incidents, as well as communication strategies and post-incident analysis. Common security mistakes—such as weak password practices, inadequate software updates, neglecting security training, poor data handling, insecure network configurations, and lack of incident response planning—can have significant impacts on an organization's security posture. Addressing these mistakes requires a proactive approach, including implementing strong security policies, educating employees, and regularly assessing and updating security practices. By understanding and mitigating these common errors, organizations can strengthen their defenses against cyber threats and enhance their overall security resilience.

Case Studies: Human Error in Major Cyber Incidents

Human error has played a significant role in numerous high-profile cyber incidents. These case studies illustrate how mistakes and oversights by individuals can lead to substantial security breaches, offering valuable lessons for improving organizational practices and mitigating similar risks in the future. Each case highlights different facets of human error, including procedural lapses, lack of awareness, and inadequate responses.

1. The Equifax Data Breach (2017)

The Equifax data breach of 2017 is a prime example of how human error can lead to massive data compromises. Equifax, one of the largest credit reporting agencies in the U.S., suffered a breach that exposed sensitive personal information of approximately 147 million people.

Details of the Incident

The breach occurred due to a failure to patch a known vulnerability in the Apache Struts web application framework. Although a patch had been released by Apache months before the breach, Equifax did not apply it in a timely manner. This lapse in patch management allowed attackers to exploit the vulnerability and access sensitive data, including Social Security numbers, birth dates, and addresses.

Human Error Factor

The human error in this case was the failure to implement the security patch. This oversight was not due to a technical malfunction but rather a procedural lapse and insufficient prioritization of critical security updates. The incident underscores the importance of timely patch management and highlights how organizational processes can impact security.

Impact and Lessons Learned

The breach led to significant financial costs, regulatory fines, and damage to Equifax's reputation. The incident prompted a reassessment of patch management practices across various industries, emphasizing the need for robust and proactive vulnerability management strategies.

2. The Target Data Breach (2013)

In 2013, retailer Target experienced a massive data breach that compromised the credit and debit card information of approximately 40 million customers. The breach also led to the exposure of personal information for an additional 70 million individuals.

Details of the Incident

The breach began with an email phishing attack targeting an employee at Target's third-party vendor, Fazio Mechanical Services. The attacker used the compromised credentials to gain access to Target's network. Once inside, the attackers deployed malware on Target's point-of-sale (POS) systems, capturing card information as transactions were processed.

Human Error Factor

The key human error in this incident was the successful phishing attack and the subsequent failure to detect and respond to the malware on POS systems. The initial compromise was due to a lack of awareness and training regarding phishing threats. Furthermore, Target's internal monitoring and response mechanisms were insufficient to identify and mitigate the attack promptly.

Impact and Lessons Learned

The breach resulted in substantial financial losses, including costs related to customer compensation, legal fees, and remediation efforts. It highlighted the importance of robust security training for employees, improved monitoring systems, and effective incident response protocols. Target's experience led to increased emphasis on securing third-party vendor relationships and enhancing overall cybersecurity resilience.

3. The Capital One Data Breach (2019)

In 2019, Capital One experienced a data breach that exposed the personal information of over 100 million customers. The breach was caused by a misconfigured web application firewall (WAF) that allowed an attacker to exploit a vulnerability and access sensitive data.

Details of the Incident

The attacker exploited a vulnerability in the WAF to gain unauthorized access to Capital One's cloud-based infrastructure, which was managed by Amazon Web Services (AWS). The misconfiguration allowed the attacker to access data stored in the cloud, including credit card applications, bank account numbers, and other personal information.

Human Error Factor

The breach was attributed to a configuration error made by a former employee who had left Capital One. This oversight involved improper settings on the WAF that failed to block unauthorized access. The error was compounded by insufficient review and monitoring of the security configurations in the cloud environment.

Impact and Lessons Learned

The breach led to significant regulatory fines, legal settlements, and reputational damage for Capital One. It underscored the critical need for thorough configuration management and continuous monitoring of cloud environments. The incident highlighted the importance of maintaining strict security controls and conducting regular audits to prevent similar errors.

4. The Sony Pictures Hack (2014)

The Sony Pictures hack in 2014 is another notable case where human error played a significant role. The attack resulted in the release of sensitive internal documents, emails, and unreleased films.

Details of the Incident

The breach was carried out by a group known as the Guardians of Peace, who used spear-phishing emails to gain access to Sony Pictures' internal network. The attackers were able to exploit weak security practices and access confidential information, including employee personal data and sensitive business communications.

Human Error Factor

The human error in this case was the susceptibility of employees to phishing attacks and the lack of adequate security training to recognize and respond to such threats. Additionally, the compromised email accounts had not been adequately protected with strong passwords or multi-factor authentication, further facilitating the attackers' access.

Impact and Lessons Learned

The hack had severe consequences for Sony Pictures, including financial losses, reputational damage, and operational disruptions. The incident highlighted the importance of implementing comprehensive security training programs, enhancing email security, and adopting multi-factor authentication to safeguard against phishing and other social engineering attacks.

5. The British Airways Data Breach (2018)

In 2018, British Airways experienced a data breach that compromised the personal and financial information of around 380,000 customers. The breach was the result of a cyber attack that exploited vulnerabilities in the airline's website and mobile app.

Details of the Incident

The attackers used a malicious script to intercept and exfiltrate customer data during the online booking process. The breach was caused by a combination of vulnerabilities in British Airways' web infrastructure and a failure to detect and address the malicious activity promptly.

Human Error Factor

The human error in this case involved lapses in monitoring and detecting the malicious script. Despite having security measures in place, British Airways failed to identify the intrusion and mitigate the impact in a timely manner. This oversight highlights the importance of continuous monitoring and threat detection capabilities.

Impact and Lessons Learned

The breach resulted in substantial financial penalties, legal actions, and customer compensation costs. It underscored the need for robust security practices, including regular security audits, enhanced monitoring systems, and prompt incident response. The incident also emphasized the importance of protecting customer data and maintaining transparency with affected individuals.

These case studies illustrate the diverse ways in which human error can contribute to major cyber incidents. By examining these incidents in detail, organizations can better understand the underlying factors that lead to security breaches and implement more effective strategies to address human-related vulnerabilities.

Summary and Key Takeaways

The exploration of major cyber incidents driven by human error reveals critical insights into the interplay between individual actions and organizational vulnerabilities. These case studies—spanning the Equifax data breach, the Target data breach, the Capital One data breach, the Sony Pictures hack, and the British Airways data breach—highlight the significant impact of human behavior on security outcomes and offer valuable lessons for improving cybersecurity practices.

Human errors, ranging from mismanagement of security patches to inadequate response to phishing attacks, have been at the core of several high-profile breaches. In each case, lapses in procedures, insufficient training, and failures in vigilance have allowed attackers to exploit weaknesses and cause substantial damage. The Equifax breach was a result of failing to apply a timely patch, while Target's breach stemmed from a phishing attack that exploited a third-party vendor. The Capital One breach involved a configuration error in cloud security settings, and the Sony Pictures hack highlighted vulnerabilities in email security and employee awareness. Lastly, the British Airways breach demonstrated the consequences of inadequate monitoring and threat detection.

Key Takeaways

1. **Timely Patching and Configuration Management**: Regular updates and proper configuration of security systems are essential to mitigate vulnerabilities. The Equifax and Capital One breaches underscore the necessity of timely application of security patches and meticulous configuration management to prevent exploitation by attackers.

2. **Comprehensive Security Training**: Effective security training programs are crucial for educating employees about potential threats such as phishing and social engineering. The Target and Sony Pictures breaches illustrate the importance of preparing employees to recognize and respond to malicious attempts, thereby reducing the risk of successful attacks.

3. **Robust Incident Detection and Response**: Continuous monitoring and swift incident response are critical in minimizing the impact of breaches. The British Airways and Sony Pictures incidents highlight the need for advanced detection mechanisms and prompt action to address and contain security threats.

4. **Third-Party Risk Management**: The Target breach illustrates the vulnerabilities that can arise from third-party vendors. Organizations must implement stringent security measures and oversight for third-party relationships to prevent them from becoming an entry point for attackers.

5. **Organizational Culture and Policy Enforcement**: Establishing a culture that prioritizes cybersecurity and enforces strong policies can significantly reduce

human-related errors. Leaders must set the tone for security practices and ensure that all employees are engaged in maintaining a secure environment.

6. **Data Protection and Compliance**: Adhering to data protection regulations and implementing robust data handling practices are essential to safeguard sensitive information. The breaches discussed highlight the financial and reputational damage that can result from inadequate data protection measures.

In conclusion, understanding the role of human error in cybersecurity incidents emphasizes the need for a holistic approach to security that includes technological solutions, human factors, and organizational practices. By addressing these areas, organizations can strengthen their defenses, reduce the risk of breaches, and enhance their overall security posture.

Suggested Readings:

Chapter 2: Building a Security-Aware Culture

2.1 Defining a Security-Aware Culture
2.2 The Importance of Leadership in Promoting Security Awareness
2.3 Strategies for Cultivating a Security-Conscious Workforce
2.4 Designing Effective Security Training Programs
2.5 Measuring and Sustaining Security Culture Improvement
2.6 Summary and Key Takeaways

Chapter 2: Building a Security-Aware Culture

In today's interconnected digital landscape, the human element is often the weakest link in an organization's security chain. Creating a security-aware culture is essential to mitigate this vulnerability. A security-aware culture emphasizes that cybersecurity is everyone's responsibility, not just that of the IT or security team. This mindset shift ensures that employees across all levels actively contribute to safeguarding the organization's assets and data.

The first step in building such a culture is comprehensive training. Organizations must provide regular, engaging, and tailored cybersecurity awareness programs. Employees should be educated about phishing attacks, password hygiene, social engineering, and the importance of reporting suspicious activities. This knowledge should be reinforced continuously through workshops, simulations, and real-world scenarios that reflect evolving threats.

Beyond education, fostering a security-aware culture requires visible leadership commitment. Executives and managers must exemplify good security practices and prioritize cybersecurity initiatives. By embedding security in organizational values and daily operations, security becomes ingrained in the workflow rather than an afterthought.

Another crucial aspect is encouraging a non-punitive reporting environment. Employees should feel comfortable reporting security incidents or mistakes without fear of punishment. This openness enables organizations to detect and address issues promptly, thereby reducing the potential impact of a breach.

Finally, organizations should reward proactive behavior in cybersecurity. Recognizing employees who demonstrate strong security practices or identify potential risks encourages others to do the same. Through continuous education, leadership involvement, and an environment of accountability and support, businesses can cultivate a robust security-aware culture that enhances overall resilience against cyber threats.

Introduction

In today's increasingly complex cybersecurity landscape, building a security-aware culture is crucial for organizations seeking to protect their assets, data, and reputation. A security-aware culture fosters an environment where security is a shared responsibility, deeply embedded in the organizational ethos, and integrated into everyday practices. This chapter explores the essential elements of cultivating a security-aware culture, including leadership commitment, employee engagement, ongoing education, and effective communication strategies.

2.1 The Importance of a Security-Aware Culture

A security-aware culture is more than just a set of policies and procedures; it reflects an organization's commitment to making security a fundamental part of its operations. Such a culture helps mitigate risks by ensuring that every member of the organization understands their role in safeguarding information and systems. The benefits of a security-aware culture include reduced risk of breaches, improved compliance with regulations, and enhanced overall security posture. According to a study by the Ponemon Institute, organizations with strong security cultures experience fewer data breaches and have lower associated costs compared to those with weaker cultures.

2.2 Leadership Commitment

2.2.1 Role of Leadership

Leadership plays a pivotal role in shaping and sustaining a security-aware culture. Leaders set the tone for security practices through their actions, decisions, and communication. A strong commitment from top executives not only drives the implementation of security initiatives but also influences employees' attitudes towards security. Leaders must champion security efforts, allocate necessary resources, and model best practices to create a culture where security is prioritized at all levels.

2.2.2 Communicating the Vision

To build a security-aware culture, leaders must clearly communicate the organization's security vision and objectives. This involves articulating the importance of security, explaining how it aligns with organizational goals, and highlighting the role of each employee in achieving security objectives. Effective communication from leadership helps establish security as a core value and ensures that security messages resonate throughout the organization.

2.3 Employee Engagement

2.3.1 Building Awareness

Employee engagement is a key component of a security-aware culture. To foster engagement, organizations should implement comprehensive security awareness programs that educate employees about potential threats, best practices, and their role in maintaining security. Programs should be interactive and tailored to address specific risks relevant to different job functions. For example, employees in finance may need to focus on protecting financial data, while those in IT may require training on secure coding practices.

2.3.2 Encouraging Participation

Active participation from employees is essential for embedding security practices into the organizational culture. Organizations can encourage participation by creating forums for discussing security issues, soliciting feedback on security policies, and involving employees in security initiatives. Recognizing and rewarding employees who demonstrate strong security practices or identify potential threats can also reinforce a security-aware culture.

2.4 Ongoing Education and Training

2.4.1 Regular Training Programs

Ongoing education is crucial for maintaining a security-aware culture. Security threats and technologies evolve rapidly, and employees need continuous training to stay informed about new risks and best practices. Regular training programs should cover a range of topics, including phishing prevention, password management, data protection, and incident response. Training should be engaging, interactive, and updated regularly to reflect current threat landscapes and security trends.

2.4.2 Simulated Attacks and Drills

Simulated attacks and security drills are effective tools for reinforcing security awareness and preparedness. By conducting phishing simulations, tabletop exercises, and incident response drills, organizations can test employees' responses to potential threats and identify areas for improvement. These exercises help employees practice their skills in a controlled environment and build confidence in their ability to handle real security incidents.

2.5 Effective Communication Strategies

2.5.1 Clear Policies and Procedures

Clear and accessible security policies and procedures are essential for guiding employees' actions and decision-making. Organizations should develop and distribute comprehensive security policies that outline acceptable use, data protection, incident reporting, and other critical areas. Policies should be written in plain language and regularly reviewed to ensure they remain relevant and effective.

2.5.2 Feedback Mechanisms

Establishing feedback mechanisms allows employees to voice concerns, report security issues, and suggest improvements. Providing channels for anonymous reporting can encourage employees to report potential threats or security lapses without fear of reprisal. Feedback from employees can help organizations identify vulnerabilities, improve security practices, and enhance overall security awareness.

2.6 Measuring and Evaluating the Culture

2.6.1 Metrics and Assessment

To gauge the effectiveness of a security-aware culture, organizations should establish metrics and conduct regular assessments. Metrics may include the frequency of security incidents, the results of phishing simulations, employee participation in training programs, and feedback from security surveys. Assessments can help organizations identify strengths and weaknesses in their security culture and guide efforts to address gaps and reinforce positive behaviors.

2.6.2 Continuous Improvement

Building a security-aware culture is an ongoing process that requires continuous improvement. Organizations should regularly review and update their security policies, training programs, and communication strategies based on feedback, assessment results, and evolving threats. By fostering a culture of continuous improvement, organizations can adapt to changing security landscapes and maintain a strong security posture. Building a security-aware culture is a fundamental aspect of effective cybersecurity. It involves leadership commitment, employee engagement, ongoing education, and effective communication strategies. By embedding security practices into the organizational culture and fostering a shared responsibility for safeguarding information, organizations can enhance their resilience against cyber threats and create a more secure environment. Through continuous effort and adaptation, organizations can maintain a robust security-aware culture that supports long-term success and protects against evolving security challenges.

Defining a Security-Aware Culture

A security-aware culture is the foundation of an organization's approach to cybersecurity. It encompasses the attitudes, behaviors, and practices that collectively shape how security is integrated into the organizational environment. Defining a security-aware culture involves understanding its core components, the role it plays in safeguarding an organization, and the strategies for fostering and sustaining it. This section explores these elements in detail, providing a comprehensive view of what constitutes a security-aware culture and why it is essential for organizational security.

1. Core Components of a Security-Aware Culture

1.1 Shared Values and Beliefs

A security-aware culture begins with a set of shared values and beliefs about the importance of cybersecurity. This involves recognizing security as a fundamental aspect of the organization's operations and a key component of its success. Employees should understand that security is not just the responsibility of the IT department but a collective responsibility that requires active participation from everyone. Shared values in a security-aware culture include:

- **Commitment to Security:** A belief that protecting information and systems is critical to the organization's success and integrity.
- **Responsibility and Accountability:** Understanding that every individual plays a role in maintaining security and is accountable for their actions.
- **Continuous Improvement:** Embracing the need for ongoing learning and adaptation to address evolving threats and vulnerabilities.

1.2 Clear Policies and Procedures

Policies and procedures form the backbone of a security-aware culture. They provide guidelines and standards for behavior, decision-making, and incident response. Effective policies should be:

- **Comprehensive:** Cover all aspects of security, including data protection, acceptable use, access controls, and incident reporting.

- **Accessible:** Clearly written in language that is easy to understand and readily available to all employees.
- **Enforced:** Regularly monitored and enforced, with clear consequences for non-compliance.

1.3 Leadership Commitment

Leadership commitment is crucial in defining and sustaining a security-aware culture. Leaders set the tone for security practices through their actions and communication. This commitment involves:

- **Visible Support:** Leaders actively demonstrate their commitment to security by participating in training, endorsing security initiatives, and making security a priority in strategic decisions.
- **Resource Allocation:** Providing adequate resources and support for security programs, including budget, tools, and personnel.
- **Communication:** Regularly communicating the importance of security and reinforcing it through consistent messaging and actions.

2. Role of a Security-Aware Culture in Safeguarding an Organization

2.1 Risk Mitigation

A security-aware culture plays a crucial role in mitigating risks by embedding security practices into daily routines and decision-making processes. Employees who are aware of security risks and know how to respond appropriately are less likely to fall victim to attacks or inadvertently contribute to security breaches. For example:

- **Phishing Awareness:** Employees who understand how to recognize and report phishing attempts can prevent attackers from gaining unauthorized access.
- **Data Protection:** Employees who follow best practices for data handling and storage reduce the risk of data breaches and leaks.

2.2 Enhanced Incident Response

A security-aware culture enhances an organization's ability to respond to incidents effectively. When employees are trained and informed about security procedures, they can act quickly and appropriately during a security incident. Key aspects include:

- **Preparedness:** Regular training and drills ensure that employees are familiar with incident response procedures and know their roles and responsibilities.

- **Communication:** Effective communication channels facilitate quick reporting and coordination during an incident.

2.3 Compliance and Governance

A security-aware culture supports compliance with regulatory requirements and governance standards. Organizations with a strong security culture are more likely to adhere to legal and regulatory obligations related to data protection and cybersecurity. This includes:

- **Policy Adherence:** Employees follow established policies and procedures, reducing the risk of non-compliance.
- **Audit Readiness:** A culture of transparency and accountability prepares organizations for internal and external audits.

3. Strategies for Fostering a Security-Aware Culture

3.1 Leadership Engagement

Engaging leadership is essential for fostering a security-aware culture. Leaders should:

- **Lead by Example:** Demonstrate commitment to security through their actions and decisions.
- **Set Clear Expectations:** Communicate security expectations and goals clearly to all employees.

- **Support Security Initiatives:** Advocate for and support security initiatives and programs.

3.2 Employee Training and Education

Ongoing training and education are vital for maintaining a security-aware culture. Effective training programs should:

- **Be Interactive and Relevant:** Use engaging methods such as simulations, scenarios, and case studies to make training relevant and memorable.
- **Address Emerging Threats:** Update training content regularly to reflect new threats and security trends.
- **Include Role-Specific Training:** Tailor training to address the specific needs and risks associated with different job functions.

3.3 Communication and Awareness

Effective communication is key to building and sustaining a security-aware culture. Strategies include:

- **Regular Updates:** Provide regular updates on security threats, best practices, and policy changes.
- **Promote Awareness Campaigns:** Use posters, newsletters, and other media to reinforce security messages and encourage vigilance.

- **Encourage Feedback:** Create channels for employees to provide feedback on security policies and report issues.

3.4 Policy Development and Enforcement

Developing and enforcing clear security policies is crucial for a security-aware culture. This involves:

- **Creating Comprehensive Policies:** Develop policies that cover all aspects of security and align with organizational goals.
- **Enforcing Compliance:** Monitor adherence to policies and take appropriate actions in cases of non-compliance.
- **Reviewing and Updating:** Regularly review and update policies to ensure they remain effective and relevant.

4. Measuring and Evaluating the Security-Aware Culture

4.1 Metrics and Indicators

To assess the effectiveness of a security-aware culture, organizations should establish metrics and indicators. These may include:

- **Incident Reports:** Track the number and types of security incidents reported by employees.

- **Training Participation:** Measure employee participation and performance in security training programs.
- **Compliance Rates:** Monitor adherence to security policies and procedures.

4.2 Surveys and Assessments

Conducting surveys and assessments can provide valuable insights into the security culture. Tools such as employee surveys, security assessments, and focus groups can help:

- **Identify Strengths and Weaknesses:** Evaluate employees' understanding of security practices and identify areas for improvement.
- **Gather Feedback:** Collect feedback on the effectiveness of training programs and communication strategies.

Defining a security-aware culture involves understanding its core components, recognizing its role in safeguarding the organization, and implementing strategies to foster and sustain it. By embedding security into organizational values, policies, and practices, and by engaging leadership and employees, organizations can build a robust security-aware culture that enhances their ability to protect against cyber threats and respond effectively to incidents. A strong security-aware culture not only mitigates risks but also supports compliance and strengthens overall organizational resilience.

The Importance of Leadership in Promoting Security Awareness

Leadership is a cornerstone in cultivating and sustaining a security-aware culture within any organization. Effective leadership shapes the organizational ethos regarding cybersecurity, sets priorities, and drives the integration of security practices into daily operations. Leaders, from executives to middle management, play a crucial role in promoting security awareness, establishing security policies, and modeling best practices. Their engagement and commitment are pivotal in embedding security into the fabric of the organization, ensuring that security becomes a shared responsibility rather than a peripheral concern.

Setting the Tone at the Top

The commitment of top executives to cybersecurity is critical in establishing a strong security posture across the organization. When leaders demonstrate a clear commitment to security, it signals its importance to all employees. This commitment involves actively participating in security initiatives, endorsing security policies, and prioritizing security in strategic decisions. For example, executives who publicly endorse security practices and allocate adequate resources for security programs reinforce the message that cybersecurity is a fundamental aspect of organizational success. This top-down approach helps in embedding security as a core value, influencing the organization's culture, and ensuring that security practices are taken seriously at all levels.

Resource Allocation and Support

Leaders are responsible for providing the resources necessary to implement and maintain effective security measures. This includes allocating budgets for security tools, technologies, and personnel. By investing in advanced security solutions, training programs, and incident response capabilities, leaders demonstrate their commitment to protecting the organization from cyber threats. Resource allocation also extends to supporting security initiatives such as regular training, security awareness campaigns, and the establishment of security teams. Adequate resources ensure that security measures are not only implemented but are also continuously updated to address evolving threats.

Developing and Enforcing Security Policies

Effective leadership involves the development and enforcement of comprehensive security policies that guide employee behavior and decision-making. Leaders must ensure that policies cover all aspects of security, including data protection, access controls, acceptable use, and incident reporting. Clear and accessible policies provide employees with the guidelines they need to make informed decisions and adhere to best practices. Additionally, leaders are responsible for enforcing these policies consistently and addressing any violations. This enforcement reinforces the importance of security practices and helps in maintaining a culture of accountability.

Communicating Security Objectives

Leaders play a key role in communicating the organization's security objectives and goals. Effective communication involves not only disseminating information about security policies and procedures but also articulating the rationale behind them. Leaders should regularly update employees on the state of cybersecurity, emerging threats, and the organization's response strategies. By communicating the importance of security and its alignment with organizational goals, leaders help employees understand their role in maintaining security and encourage them to adopt security-conscious behaviors.

Modeling Best Practices

Leaders set an example for employees by modeling best practices in cybersecurity. Their behavior, from using strong passwords and following data protection protocols to reporting suspicious activities, serves as a powerful demonstration of security commitment. When leaders consistently adhere to security practices and address security issues promptly, they reinforce the importance of these behaviors for all employees. This modeling helps in creating a culture where security is ingrained in everyday actions and decisions.

Promoting a Security-First Mindset

A security-first mindset is essential for building a security-aware culture, and leaders are instrumental in fostering this mindset. By prioritizing security in strategic planning, decision-making, and operations, leaders ensure that security considerations are integrated into all aspects of the organization. This involves viewing security as an ongoing process rather than a one-time effort, encouraging continuous learning and adaptation to new threats. Leaders who emphasize the importance of proactive security measures, such as regular risk assessments and vulnerability testing, help in creating a culture of vigilance and resilience.

Engaging Employees and Building Trust

Leadership engagement is also crucial for building trust and encouraging employee participation in security initiatives.

Leaders should actively involve employees in security efforts by soliciting their feedback, addressing their concerns, and recognizing their contributions to security. Creating a supportive environment where employees feel empowered to report security issues and suggest improvements fosters a collaborative approach to security. Leaders who engage with employees and show appreciation for their efforts help in building a culture where security is a shared responsibility. The role of leadership in promoting security awareness cannot be overstated. Leaders set the tone for security practices, allocate resources, develop and enforce policies, communicate objectives, model best practices, and foster a security-first mindset. Their engagement and commitment are essential for embedding security into the organizational culture, ensuring that security is prioritized and maintained at all levels. By actively supporting and participating in security initiatives, leaders help in creating a robust security-aware culture that enhances the organization's ability to protect against cyber threats and respond effectively to incidents.

Strategies for Cultivating a Security-Conscious Workforce

Cultivating a security-conscious workforce is vital for defending against cyber threats and ensuring the integrity and confidentiality of organizational data. Employees are often the first line of defense against security breaches, making their awareness and adherence to security practices crucial. Developing a workforce that is proactive, knowledgeable, and vigilant about cybersecurity requires a multifaceted approach involving training, communication, engagement, and reinforcement. This section outlines effective strategies for building a security-conscious workforce, highlighting key practices and techniques to enhance overall security posture.

1. Comprehensive Security Training Programs

1.1 Interactive and Engaging Training

Effective security training goes beyond basic awareness and involves interactive and engaging methods that capture employees' attention. Training programs should incorporate simulations, role-playing scenarios, and case studies to provide practical experience in handling security threats. For instance, phishing simulation exercises can help employees recognize and respond to phishing attempts in a controlled environment, enhancing their ability to identify real threats.

1.2 Role-Specific Training

Tailoring training to specific job roles and responsibilities ensures that employees receive relevant information pertinent to their tasks. For example, IT staff may need advanced training on secure coding practices and vulnerability management, while finance employees might focus on safeguarding financial data and recognizing financial fraud. Role-specific training helps employees understand the unique risks associated with their positions and how to mitigate them effectively.

1.3 Regular Updates and Refresher Courses

Cybersecurity is a constantly evolving field, and regular updates and refresher courses are necessary to keep employees informed about new threats and best practices. Training programs should be updated periodically to reflect the latest security trends, threat intelligence, and regulatory requirements. Implementing a continuous learning approach helps employees stay current and maintain a high level of security awareness.

2. Strong Communication Channels

2.1 Clear and Consistent Messaging

Effective communication is essential for reinforcing security practices and ensuring that employees understand the importance of cybersecurity. Organizations should develop clear and consistent messaging regarding security policies, procedures, and expectations. Regular communication through emails, newsletters, and intranet updates helps keep security at the forefront of employees' minds and reinforces key security messages.

2.2 Security Awareness Campaigns

Running security awareness campaigns can enhance employees' understanding of security risks and promote best practices. Campaigns can include posters, flyers, and digital signage that highlight common threats, security tips, and the importance of adhering to security policies. Interactive elements such as quizzes and contests can make these campaigns more engaging and memorable.

2.3 Feedback Mechanisms

Establishing feedback mechanisms allows employees to report security concerns, provide suggestions, and seek clarification on security issues. Providing channels for anonymous reporting can encourage employees to voice their concerns without fear of reprisal. Regularly reviewing feedback and addressing concerns helps organizations identify potential vulnerabilities and improve security practices.

3. Building a Security-First Culture

3.1 Leadership Support and Example

Leaders play a crucial role in fostering a security-first culture by demonstrating their commitment to security practices and setting a positive example. Leaders should actively participate in security training, adhere to security policies, and support security initiatives. Their visible support reinforces the importance of security and encourages employees to prioritize cybersecurity in their daily activities.

3.2 Integrating Security into Performance Metrics

Incorporating security into performance metrics and evaluations helps reinforce the importance of cybersecurity and encourages employees to take ownership of their security responsibilities. For example, including security-related goals in performance reviews and recognizing employees who demonstrate strong security practices can motivate staff to prioritize security.

3.3 Creating a Sense of Ownership

Fostering a sense of ownership among employees encourages them to take an active role in maintaining security. Involving employees in security initiatives, such as participating in security committees or leading security awareness activities, helps them feel more invested in the organization's security efforts. Providing opportunities for employees to contribute to security discussions and decision-making can also enhance their sense of responsibility.

4. Implementing Security Policies and Procedures

4.1 Clear and Accessible Policies

Developing clear and accessible security policies is essential for guiding employees' behavior and decision-making. Policies should cover all aspects of security, including acceptable use, data protection, access controls, and incident reporting. Ensuring that policies are easily accessible and written in plain language helps employees understand and adhere to security guidelines.

4.2 Enforcement and Compliance

Enforcing security policies and procedures is crucial for maintaining a security-conscious workforce. Organizations should monitor compliance with security policies, conduct regular audits, and address any violations promptly. Implementing a structured approach to policy enforcement helps reinforce the importance of security and ensures that employees adhere to established guidelines.

5. Encouraging Proactive Security Behaviors

5.1 Empowering Employees to Report Threats

Encouraging employees to report potential security threats and incidents promptly helps organizations detect and address issues before they escalate. Providing clear instructions on how to report suspicious activities and creating a supportive environment for reporting helps employees feel confident in their ability to contribute to security.

5.2 Recognizing and Rewarding Good Practices

Recognizing and rewarding employees who demonstrate strong security practices and contribute to maintaining a secure environment helps reinforce positive behaviors. Implementing recognition programs, such as awards or incentives for employees who identify and report security issues, encourages a proactive approach to cybersecurity.

5.3 Promoting Security Awareness as a Shared Responsibility

Emphasizing that security is a shared responsibility among all employees helps create a collective commitment to maintaining a secure environment. Encouraging collaboration and information sharing among departments and teams can enhance overall security awareness and foster a culture of vigilance. Cultivating a security-conscious workforce involves implementing comprehensive training programs, establishing strong communication channels, building a security-first culture, and enforcing security policies and procedures. By engaging employees through interactive training, clear communication, and recognition of good practices, organizations can enhance their overall security posture and reduce the risk of cyber threats. A proactive, knowledgeable, and vigilant workforce is essential for maintaining a robust security environment and protecting organizational assets from evolving cyber threats.

Designing Effective Security Training Programs

Designing effective security training programs is crucial for fostering a security-conscious workforce and mitigating the risks associated with cyber threats. Security training should be more than a mere formality; it must be engaging, relevant, and tailored to the specific needs of the organization and its employees. A well-designed training program not only educates employees about potential threats and security best practices but also empowers them to act proactively in maintaining a secure environment. This section outlines the key components and strategies for designing effective security training programs that enhance overall organizational security.

1. Assessing Training Needs

1.1 Identifying Specific Risks and Requirements

Before developing a training program, it is essential to assess the specific risks and requirements of the organization. This involves identifying the types of data and systems that need protection, understanding the threat landscape, and evaluating the current level of security awareness among employees. Conducting a risk assessment and reviewing past security incidents can provide valuable insights into the areas that require focus in the training program.

1.2 Defining Target Audiences

Different job roles and departments within an organization face unique security challenges. Tailoring the training program to address the needs of various target audiences ensures that the content is relevant and applicable. For example, IT staff may require advanced training on network security and incident response, while general employees may need foundational training on recognizing phishing emails and following data protection practices.

2. Developing Engaging and Interactive Content

2.1 Utilizing Diverse Training Methods

To maintain engagement and enhance learning, security training programs should incorporate a variety of training methods. These methods may include:

- **Interactive E-Learning Modules:** Online courses that use multimedia elements such as videos, quizzes, and simulations to deliver content in an engaging format.

- **Classroom Training:** Instructor-led sessions that provide opportunities for hands-on practice and real-time interaction with trainers.
- **Workshops and Seminars:** Specialized sessions focusing on specific topics or recent threats, often led by external experts or industry professionals.

2.2 Real-World Scenarios and Simulations

Incorporating real-world scenarios and simulations into training helps employees apply theoretical knowledge to practical situations. Simulations such as phishing exercises, simulated cyberattacks, and breach response drills allow employees to practice their skills in a controlled environment. These activities can enhance their ability to recognize and respond to actual threats effectively.

2.3 Role-Specific Training

Customizing training content for different job roles ensures that employees receive information relevant to their specific responsibilities. Role-specific training may include:

- **Phishing Awareness:** Training focused on recognizing phishing attempts and avoiding social engineering attacks, suitable for all employees.

- **Data Protection:** Training for employees handling sensitive data, emphasizing data encryption, access controls, and secure data storage practices.
- **Incident Response:** Advanced training for IT and security staff on detecting, responding to, and mitigating security incidents.

3. Implementing Training Programs

3.1 Creating a Structured Training Plan

A well-structured training plan outlines the training objectives, content, methods, and schedule. The plan should include:

- **Learning Objectives:** Clearly defined goals that specify what employees should know or be able to do after completing the training.
- **Content Outline:** A detailed outline of the topics to be covered, including key concepts, policies, and procedures.
- **Training Schedule:** A timeline for delivering the training, including frequency and duration of sessions.

3.2 Delivering Training Effectively

Effective delivery of training is crucial for ensuring that employees absorb and retain the information. Strategies for effective delivery include:

- **Engaging Presenters:** Using skilled trainers who can present content clearly and interactively.
- **Interactive Elements:** Incorporating discussions, Q&A sessions, and hands-on activities to facilitate engagement and understanding.
- **Feedback Mechanisms:** Providing opportunities for employees to ask questions and receive feedback on their performance.

4. Evaluating and Enhancing Training Programs

4.1 Measuring Training Effectiveness

Evaluating the effectiveness of security training programs is essential for continuous improvement. Key metrics to assess include:

- **Knowledge Retention:** Testing employees' understanding of key concepts through quizzes and assessments.
- **Behavioral Changes:** Monitoring changes in employee behavior, such as improved adherence to security policies and reduced incidents of security breaches.
- **Incident Reduction:** Tracking the frequency and severity of security incidents before and after training to gauge its impact.

4.2 Gathering Feedback and Making Improvements

Collecting feedback from employees and stakeholders can provide insights into the strengths and weaknesses of the training program. Surveys, interviews, and focus groups can help identify areas for improvement and ensure that the training remains relevant and effective. Regularly reviewing and updating training content based on feedback, new threats, and emerging best practices ensures that the program stays current and continues to meet the organization's needs.

5. Promoting Continuous Learning

5.1 Ongoing Education and Refreshers

Security training should be an ongoing process rather than a one-time event. Providing periodic refresher courses and updates on new threats and technologies helps reinforce security knowledge and keep employees informed about the latest developments. Regular training helps maintain a high level of security awareness and ensures that employees are prepared to handle evolving threats.

5.2 Creating a Learning Culture

Fostering a culture of continuous learning and improvement encourages employees to stay engaged with security practices and take responsibility for their own learning. Encouraging self-directed learning, offering access to additional resources, and supporting professional development opportunities in cybersecurity can help employees stay informed and motivated. Designing effective security training programs involves assessing training needs, developing engaging content, implementing structured training, and evaluating its effectiveness. By utilizing diverse training methods, tailoring content to specific roles, and promoting continuous learning, organizations can build a security-conscious workforce capable of defending against cyber threats and maintaining a secure environment. A well-designed training program not only enhances employees' knowledge and skills but also fosters a culture of security awareness and responsibility throughout the organization.

Measuring and Sustaining Security Culture Improvement

Measuring and sustaining security culture improvement is critical for ensuring that cybersecurity practices are deeply embedded within an organization. A security-aware culture is one where every employee understands their role in maintaining security and actively participates in safeguarding the organization's assets. This section outlines the methodologies and strategies for assessing the effectiveness of security culture initiatives and maintaining ongoing improvements to foster a robust security environment.

1. Measuring Security Culture Improvement

1.1 Establishing Key Performance Indicators (KPIs)

Key Performance Indicators (KPIs) are essential for evaluating the effectiveness of security culture initiatives. These metrics provide quantitative and qualitative data on various aspects of security awareness and behavior. Common KPIs include:

- **Incident Frequency:** Tracking the number of security incidents or breaches over time to assess whether improvements in security culture are leading to a reduction in incidents.
- **Employee Training Completion Rates:** Measuring the percentage of employees who complete security training programs and any follow-up training sessions.
- **Compliance Rates:** Monitoring adherence to security policies and procedures, such as password policies and data protection guidelines.
- **Phishing Test Results:** Analyzing the results of simulated phishing tests to gauge employees' ability to recognize and respond to phishing attempts.

By regularly reviewing these KPIs, organizations can assess the impact of their security culture initiatives and identify areas that require further attention or improvement.

1.2 Conducting Security Culture Surveys

Security culture surveys are a valuable tool for gaining insights into employees' perceptions, attitudes, and behaviors related to cybersecurity. Surveys can include questions on:

- **Awareness Levels:** Assessing employees' knowledge of security policies, procedures, and best practices.
- **Behavioral Practices:** Evaluating how employees apply security practices in their daily work and whether they follow established protocols.
- **Perceived Importance of Security:** Understanding employees' views on the importance of security and their level of commitment to maintaining a secure environment.

Survey results provide actionable data that can inform targeted interventions and help organizations measure progress in enhancing security culture. To ensure reliability, surveys should be conducted periodically and anonymized to encourage honest feedback.

1.3 Analyzing Incident Reports and Metrics

Analyzing incident reports and security metrics helps in understanding the effectiveness of security culture improvements. This analysis involves:

- **Reviewing Incident Reports:** Examining the nature, frequency, and impact of security incidents to identify trends and potential weaknesses in security practices.
- **Benchmarking Performance:** Comparing performance metrics against industry standards or previous periods to evaluate progress and identify areas for enhancement.

By analyzing these data points, organizations can gain insights into how security culture improvements are translating into reduced incidents and better overall security performance.

2. Sustaining Security Culture Improvement

2.1 Continuous Training and Education

Ongoing training and education are essential for sustaining improvements in security culture. This involves:

- **Regular Refresher Courses:** Providing periodic refresher courses to reinforce security knowledge and update employees on new threats and best practices.

- **Advanced Training Opportunities:** Offering advanced training for employees with specialized roles or responsibilities, such as IT staff or data handlers, to ensure they stay current with evolving security challenges.

Continuous training helps keep security at the forefront of employees' minds and reinforces their commitment to maintaining a secure environment.

2.2 Leadership and Communication

Effective leadership and communication play a crucial role in sustaining security culture improvements. Key strategies include:

- **Visible Leadership Commitment:** Leaders should actively demonstrate their commitment to security by participating in training, enforcing policies, and communicating the importance of security practices.
- **Regular Communication:** Keeping employees informed about security updates, recent threats, and best practices through regular communications such as newsletters, meetings, and intranet updates.

By maintaining open lines of communication and demonstrating leadership commitment, organizations can reinforce the importance of security and ensure ongoing engagement with security culture initiatives.

2.3 Encouraging Employee Engagement and Ownership

Fostering a sense of ownership and engagement among employees is vital for sustaining security culture improvements. Strategies include:

- **Recognizing and Rewarding Good Practices:** Implementing recognition programs that reward employees for demonstrating strong security practices and contributing to a secure environment.
- **Involving Employees in Security Initiatives:** Encouraging employees to participate in security committees, provide feedback on security policies, and contribute to security awareness campaigns.

Engaging employees and making them feel like active participants in security efforts helps maintain their commitment and reinforces the importance of security practices.

2.4 Reviewing and Updating Security Policies

Regularly reviewing and updating security policies and procedures ensures they remain relevant and effective. This involves:

- **Periodic Policy Reviews:** Conducting periodic reviews of security policies to ensure they align with current threats, regulatory requirements, and organizational changes.

- **Incorporating Feedback:** Integrating feedback from employees and stakeholders into policy updates to address any gaps or areas for improvement.

By keeping policies up to date and relevant, organizations can ensure that security practices continue to meet the needs of the organization and its employees.

2.5 Leveraging Technology and Tools

Utilizing technology and tools can support the maintenance of a strong security culture. Key approaches include:

- **Automated Training Systems:** Implementing automated training systems that deliver targeted security training and track employee progress.
- **Security Dashboards:** Using security dashboards to provide real-time visibility into security metrics, incidents, and compliance status.

These tools help streamline security management and provide valuable insights into the effectiveness of security culture initiatives.

Measuring and sustaining security culture improvement involves a comprehensive approach that includes establishing KPIs, conducting surveys, analyzing metrics, and maintaining ongoing training and communication. By continuously evaluating and refining security culture initiatives, organizations can ensure that their security practices remain effective and that employees remain engaged and committed to maintaining a secure environment. Sustaining a strong security culture is an ongoing effort that requires active leadership, employee involvement, and the strategic use of technology and tools. Through these efforts, organizations can build a resilient security culture capable of adapting to evolving threats and safeguarding critical assets.

Summary and Key Takeaways

In the realm of cybersecurity, a robust and dynamic security culture is crucial for safeguarding organizational assets and mitigating risks. The measurement and sustainability of security culture improvement involve a multi-faceted approach, incorporating diverse strategies and continuous efforts to foster a security-aware environment. Effective security culture initiatives not only educate employees about potential threats and best practices but also ensure their active engagement and adherence to security protocols.

The process of measuring security culture improvement begins with establishing Key Performance Indicators (KPIs) that offer quantitative and qualitative insights into the effectiveness of security initiatives. KPIs such as incident frequency, training completion rates, and compliance rates provide valuable data for assessing progress. Conducting security culture surveys further aids in understanding employees' perceptions and behaviors related to cybersecurity. These surveys offer actionable feedback that can be used to refine training programs and security practices. Additionally, analyzing incident reports and security metrics helps in identifying trends and assessing the impact of security culture improvements on organizational security.

Sustaining security culture improvement requires a continuous commitment to training and education. Regular refresher courses, advanced training opportunities, and ongoing updates ensure that employees remain informed about evolving threats and best practices. Effective leadership and communication play a significant role in reinforcing the importance of security practices and maintaining engagement. Leaders must visibly support security initiatives and communicate regularly with employees about security updates and best practices. Encouraging employee engagement and ownership through recognition programs and involvement in security initiatives helps reinforce commitment and accountability.

Regularly reviewing and updating security policies ensures that they remain relevant and effective in addressing current threats and organizational changes. Leveraging technology and tools, such as automated training systems and security dashboards, supports the maintenance of a strong security culture by providing valuable insights and streamlining security management.

Key Takeaways

1. **Establish KPIs for Effective Measurement:**
    - Implement Key Performance Indicators (KPIs) to monitor security culture initiatives, including metrics such as incident frequency, employee training completion rates, and compliance rates. These KPIs provide actionable data for assessing the effectiveness of security programs and identifying areas for improvement.
2. **Conduct Regular Security Culture Surveys:**
    - Use surveys to gain insights into employees' perceptions, attitudes, and behaviors related to cybersecurity. Regular surveys help in understanding the impact of security culture initiatives and identifying areas that require further attention.

3. **Analyze Incident Reports and Metrics:**
    - Review and analyze incident reports and security metrics to identify trends and evaluate the effectiveness of security culture improvements. Benchmarking performance against industry standards or previous periods helps in assessing progress and making data-driven decisions.
4. **Provide Continuous Training and Education:**
    - Implement ongoing training programs, including refresher courses and advanced training, to keep employees informed about new threats and best practices. Continuous education ensures that security awareness remains high and employees are prepared to handle evolving challenges.
5. **Foster Effective Leadership and Communication:**
    - Ensure that leaders actively support security initiatives and communicate regularly with employees about security updates and practices. Leadership commitment and effective communication reinforce the

importance of security and maintain employee engagement.

6. **Encourage Employee Engagement and Ownership:**
    o Recognize and reward employees for demonstrating strong security practices and involving them in security initiatives. Creating a sense of ownership and responsibility among employees enhances their commitment to maintaining a secure environment.

7. **Regularly Review and Update Security Policies:**
    o Conduct periodic reviews of security policies to ensure they align with current threats, regulatory requirements, and organizational changes. Integrate feedback from employees and stakeholders to address any gaps or areas for improvement.

8. **Leverage Technology and Tools:**
    o Utilize automated training systems and security dashboards to streamline security management and provide real-time visibility into security metrics. Technology tools support the maintenance of a strong security

culture and facilitate data-driven decision-making.

By implementing these strategies, organizations can build and sustain a security-conscious workforce, effectively managing risks and enhancing their overall security posture. A strong security culture is an ongoing effort that requires continuous evaluation, engagement, and adaptation to safeguard against emerging threats and ensure the protection of critical assets.

Chapter 3: Training and Education for Cybersecurity Awareness

3.1 Developing Comprehensive Security Training Programs
3.2 Creating Engaging and Interactive Training Materials
3.3 The Role of Regular Security Awareness Campaigns
3.4 Evaluating Training Effectiveness and Impact
3.5 Adapting Training for Different Roles and Skill Levels
3.6 Summary and Key Takeaways

Chapter 3: Training and Education for Cybersecurity Awareness

Introduction

Effective training and education are fundamental components of a robust cybersecurity strategy. As the threat landscape evolves and cyber-attacks become increasingly sophisticated, the need for a well-informed and vigilant workforce has never been more critical. This chapter delves into the essential elements of cybersecurity training and education, exploring strategies to enhance employee awareness, the development of targeted training programs, and the integration of continuous learning to foster a culture of security within an organization.

Developing a Comprehensive Training Program

Creating a comprehensive cybersecurity training program involves a systematic approach to ensure that all employees are equipped with the necessary knowledge and skills to recognize and mitigate potential threats. A well-structured training program should start with a thorough assessment of the organization's specific needs, including an analysis of the types of data and systems that require protection, as well as an understanding of the common threats faced by the organization. This assessment helps in designing a training curriculum that is relevant and tailored to the unique needs of the organization and its employees.

The training program should be designed to cover a broad range of topics, including fundamental cybersecurity principles, common threats such as phishing and malware, and best practices for securing sensitive information. It is essential to utilize diverse training methods to cater to different learning styles and keep employees engaged. Interactive e-learning modules, instructor-led workshops, and hands-on simulations are effective methods for delivering training content in an engaging and practical manner. Additionally, incorporating real-world scenarios and case studies helps employees apply their knowledge to practical situations, reinforcing the importance of adhering to security practices.

Personalizing Training for Different Roles

One of the key aspects of an effective cybersecurity training program is its ability to address the specific needs of different job roles within the organization. Different roles face different security challenges, and tailored training ensures that employees receive relevant information that directly impacts their responsibilities. For example, IT staff may require advanced training on network security and incident response, while general employees may need foundational training on recognizing phishing attempts and secure password practices.

Role-specific training helps ensure that employees are not overwhelmed with information that is not applicable to their roles, making the training more effective and engaging. It is also important to provide specialized training for employees who handle sensitive data or have access to critical systems, as these individuals play a crucial role in maintaining the organization's security posture.

Implementing Continuous Learning and Awareness Programs

Cybersecurity threats are constantly evolving, and it is crucial for training programs to adapt to these changes. Continuous learning and awareness programs help keep employees informed about the latest threats, vulnerabilities, and best practices. Regular refresher courses, updates on new security trends, and periodic security drills are essential components of an ongoing training strategy. Incorporating a culture of continuous learning involves more than just periodic training sessions; it requires integrating security awareness into the daily routines of employees. This can be achieved through various methods such as security newsletters, regular updates on recent threats, and interactive quizzes or challenges that reinforce key concepts. Encouraging employees to stay informed and engaged with security practices helps maintain a high level of awareness and readiness to address emerging threats.

Evaluating Training Effectiveness

Measuring the effectiveness of cybersecurity training programs is essential to ensure that they are achieving their intended goals. Evaluations should focus on several key areas, including knowledge retention, changes in behavior, and the impact on overall security posture. Various assessment tools such as quizzes, surveys, and practical exercises can be used to gauge employees' understanding and application of security concepts.

Feedback from employees is also valuable in evaluating the effectiveness of training programs. Conducting surveys and interviews to gather insights into employees' perceptions of the training content, delivery methods, and overall experience can provide actionable data for improving the program. Additionally, monitoring key performance indicators such as incident rates, compliance levels, and response times can help assess the impact of training on the organization's security posture.

Promoting a Security Culture through Education

Education plays a crucial role in fostering a security-conscious culture within an organization. A security-aware culture is one where employees understand the importance of cybersecurity and are proactive in protecting organizational assets. To promote this culture, it is important to integrate security education into the organization's core values and practices.

Leadership plays a key role in promoting a security culture by setting the tone at the top and demonstrating a commitment to security through their actions and communications. Encouraging employees to take ownership of their role in maintaining security and recognizing their contributions to the organization's security efforts helps reinforce the importance of cybersecurity.

Additionally, creating opportunities for employees to engage in security-related discussions, participate in security events, and contribute to security initiatives can help build a sense of community and shared responsibility. By making cybersecurity a central part of the organizational culture, employees are more likely to stay engaged and motivated to follow best practices.

Training and education are critical elements of an effective cybersecurity strategy, essential for equipping employees with the knowledge and skills needed to protect organizational assets. Developing a comprehensive and tailored training program, implementing continuous learning initiatives, and evaluating the effectiveness of training efforts are key components of building a security-aware culture. By fostering ongoing education and promoting a culture of security, organizations can enhance their overall security posture and better protect themselves against the ever-evolving landscape of cyber threats.

3.2 Creating Engaging and Interactive Training Materials

Creating engaging and interactive training materials is essential for effective cybersecurity education. Traditional methods of training, such as lengthy presentations or text-heavy documents, often fail to captivate and motivate employees. To ensure that cybersecurity training is not only informative but also engaging, it is crucial to develop materials that actively involve learners and make the content memorable. This section explores various strategies and techniques for designing interactive training materials that enhance learning outcomes and foster a deeper understanding of cybersecurity concepts.

1. Leveraging Multimedia Elements

1.1 Incorporating Videos and Animations

Multimedia elements, such as videos and animations, can significantly enhance the engagement and effectiveness of cybersecurity training materials. Videos can be used to introduce key concepts, demonstrate real-world scenarios, and provide visual explanations of complex topics. Animated graphics and simulations can visually represent abstract concepts and processes, making them easier to understand. For instance, animations that illustrate how a phishing attack unfolds or how malware spreads can provide a clearer understanding of these threats.

To maximize their impact, videos and animations should be concise, high-quality, and tailored to the target audience. They should also be supplemented with clear explanations and practical examples to reinforce the learning objectives.

1.2 Utilizing Interactive Infographics

Interactive infographics combine visual appeal with interactive elements, allowing learners to explore information at their own pace. Infographics can be used to present statistics, processes, or security best practices in a visually engaging manner. Interactive features, such as clickable elements, pop-up windows, or hover-over text, enable users to access additional details or explanations as needed.

For example, an interactive infographic on data protection might allow users to click on different types of data breaches to learn more about their impact and prevention measures. This interactive approach helps learners engage with the content more actively and retain information more effectively.

2. Incorporating Gamification Techniques

2.1 Designing Interactive Quizzes and Assessments

Gamification techniques, such as interactive quizzes and assessments, can make learning more engaging and enjoyable. Quizzes and assessments provide learners with opportunities to test their knowledge, reinforce key concepts, and receive immediate feedback. Well-designed quizzes can include various question formats, such as multiple-choice, true/false, and scenario-based questions, to assess different aspects of cybersecurity knowledge.

Incorporating elements of competition, such as leaderboards or timed challenges, can further motivate learners to participate actively and strive for better performance. For example, a cybersecurity training module might feature a quiz where employees compete to identify phishing emails or solve security-related puzzles.

2.2 Implementing Simulation Games

Simulation games immerse learners in realistic scenarios, allowing them to apply their knowledge in a controlled environment. These games can simulate various cybersecurity situations, such as responding to a security breach, managing a network security incident, or handling a phishing attack. By engaging in these simulations, learners can practice their skills, make decisions, and see the consequences of their actions in real-time.

Simulation games can be designed to include different levels of difficulty, allowing learners to progress from basic to advanced scenarios. They also provide valuable hands-on experience and help build confidence in applying cybersecurity concepts.

3. Developing Role-Specific Training Scenarios

3.1 Creating Tailored Scenarios for Different Roles

Role-specific training scenarios ensure that the content is relevant to employees' specific job functions and responsibilities. For example, IT staff might receive training on advanced topics such as network security protocols and incident response, while general employees might focus on recognizing phishing attempts and securing personal data.

Tailored scenarios should reflect the types of threats and challenges that employees are likely to encounter in their roles. For instance, a scenario for finance employees might involve detecting fraudulent transactions, while a scenario for customer service representatives could focus on handling sensitive customer information securely.

3.2 Incorporating Real-World Case Studies

Incorporating real-world case studies into training materials provides practical examples of how cybersecurity concepts are applied in real situations. Case studies can highlight notable security incidents, discuss the factors that contributed to the breaches, and analyze the response and resolution.

For example, a case study might examine a high-profile data breach, detailing the methods used by the attackers, the vulnerabilities exploited, and the lessons learned. By analyzing real-world cases, learners can gain insights into effective security practices and understand the importance of vigilance and preparedness.

4. Facilitating Interactive Learning Experiences

4.1 Implementing Virtual Labs and Hands-On Exercises

Virtual labs and hands-on exercises provide learners with practical experience in a simulated environment. Virtual labs allow employees to practice cybersecurity skills, such as configuring security settings, analyzing network traffic, or performing vulnerability assessments, without risking real systems. These exercises offer a safe space to experiment and develop proficiency in applying security techniques.

Hands-on exercises can be integrated into training modules to reinforce theoretical knowledge and provide practical experience. For example, an exercise might involve analyzing a simulated phishing email to identify signs of phishing and practice appropriate response actions.

4.2 Encouraging Collaborative Learning

Collaborative learning activities, such as group discussions, team-based exercises, and peer reviews, foster interaction and knowledge sharing among employees. Collaborative learning helps learners benefit from each other's experiences, perspectives, and expertise.

For example, a training workshop might include group activities where employees work together to solve security challenges, share their solutions, and discuss best practices.

Collaborative learning encourages active participation and enhances the overall learning experience. Creating engaging and interactive training materials is essential for effective cybersecurity education. By leveraging multimedia elements, incorporating gamification techniques, developing role-specific scenarios, and facilitating interactive learning experiences, organizations can enhance the effectiveness of their training programs and foster a deeper understanding of cybersecurity concepts. Engaging training materials not only capture learners' attention but also promote active participation and long-term retention of critical security knowledge. Ultimately, well-designed training materials contribute to building a security-conscious workforce capable of effectively defending against evolving cyber threats.

The Role of Regular Security Awareness Campaigns

Regular security awareness campaigns play a pivotal role in reinforcing cybersecurity practices and fostering a culture of vigilance within an organization. These campaigns are designed to keep employees informed about emerging threats, best practices, and the importance of adhering to security policies. By maintaining a continuous dialogue about security, organizations can ensure that employees remain engaged, knowledgeable, and prepared to handle potential cyber risks. This section explores the significance of regular security awareness campaigns, highlighting key strategies for their implementation and providing examples of how coding and technology can be integrated to enhance these efforts.

1. Importance of Consistent Messaging

1.1 Reinforcing Security Practices

Consistent messaging through regular security awareness campaigns helps reinforce security practices and keeps them top-of-mind for employees. Regularly communicating about security topics ensures that employees do not become complacent and remain vigilant against potential threats. Campaigns can include updates on recent security incidents, new threats, and reminders of best practices. For instance, periodic emails or newsletters can provide information on secure password practices, phishing prevention, and data protection.

An example of reinforcing secure practices could be a monthly email update featuring a "Security Tip of the Month," where employees receive actionable advice on how to protect their accounts and data. This can be accompanied by coding examples such as proper password hashing techniques, emphasizing the importance of using secure algorithms in their own development practices:

```
def hash_password(password: str) -> str:
    # Using SHA-256 to hash the password
    return hashlib.sha256(password.encode()).hexdigest()

# Example usage
password = 'SecureP@ssw0rd'
hashed_password = hash_password(password)
print(f'Hashed Password: {hashed_password}')
```

By providing such coding examples, organizations not only reinforce security practices but also educate employees on secure coding techniques, aligning with best practices in software development.

1.2 Enhancing Awareness of Emerging Threats

Cybersecurity threats are continually evolving, making it essential for employees to stay informed about new and emerging risks. Regular awareness campaigns can highlight recent developments in the threat landscape, such as new types of malware, phishing tactics, or vulnerabilities. For instance, a quarterly security bulletin could feature detailed analyses of recent cyber incidents, including how they occurred and the lessons learned.

In addition to textual updates, campaigns can use interactive elements such as simulations of new phishing tactics or malware. For example, a simulated phishing campaign might involve sending out mock phishing emails to employees to test their ability to recognize and report such threats. This practical approach helps employees learn how to identify and respond to phishing attempts effectively.

2. Leveraging Technology and Tools

2.1 Integrating Interactive Tools and Simulations

Interactive tools and simulations are effective in making security awareness campaigns more engaging and informative. Tools such as interactive quizzes, security games, and simulated attack scenarios provide employees with hands-on experience in identifying and responding to security threats. For example, an interactive quiz might test employees' knowledge of phishing signs and secure email practices, while a simulated attack scenario could involve a mock ransomware attack that employees must navigate.

Incorporating coding exercises into these tools can provide a practical aspect to the training. For example, a simulation might involve a coding challenge where employees must identify and fix security vulnerabilities in a piece of sample code. Here's an example of a simple coding vulnerability that employees might be tasked with identifying and fixing:

Vulnerable Code Example

```python
import os

def delete_file(file_name):
    os.remove(file_name)

# Example usage
delete_file('/path/to/file.txt')
```

In this example, employees would need to recognize the potential risk of directory traversal attacks and modify the code to include proper validation and security checks:

```python
# Secure Code Example
import os

def delete_file(file_name):
    # Validate the file path to prevent directory traversal attacks
    if '..' in file_name or file_name.startswith('/'):
        raise ValueError("Invalid file path")
    os.remove(file_name)

# Example usage
delete_file('file.txt')
```

By incorporating such practical exercises, employees can gain valuable insights into secure coding practices and enhance their overall security awareness.

2.2 Utilizing Data Analytics for Campaign Effectiveness

Data analytics can play a crucial role in evaluating the effectiveness of security awareness campaigns. By analyzing metrics such as participation rates, quiz scores, incident reporting rates, and feedback surveys, organizations can assess the impact of their campaigns and identify areas for improvement. For example, tracking the success rate of simulated phishing exercises can provide insights into how well employees are learning to recognize phishing attempts.

Organizations can also use data analytics to tailor campaigns based on employee performance and engagement. For instance, if a particular department consistently scores lower on security quizzes, targeted training sessions can be developed to address their specific knowledge gaps. By leveraging data analytics, organizations can continuously refine their awareness campaigns and ensure they meet the needs of their employees.

3. Encouraging Active Participation and Engagement

3.1 Creating Interactive Learning Experiences

Encouraging active participation and engagement is essential for the success of security awareness campaigns. Interactive learning experiences, such as gamified training modules and team-based challenges, can make learning more enjoyable and effective. For instance, a cybersecurity escape room game might involve solving security-related puzzles and challenges to "escape" from a simulated attack scenario.

In addition to gamified experiences, creating opportunities for employees to contribute to security discussions and initiatives can further enhance engagement. For example, organizing security-themed hackathons or inviting employees to share their experiences and solutions to security challenges can foster a sense of community and collaboration.

3.2 Recognizing and Rewarding Security Efforts

Recognizing and rewarding employees for their efforts in maintaining security awareness can further motivate participation and adherence to best practices. Implementing recognition programs, such as "Security Champion" awards or monthly shout-outs for employees who demonstrate exceptional security practices, can reinforce positive behavior and encourage others to follow suit.

Rewarding employees for participating in security training, successfully completing quizzes, or identifying potential security threats can help create a culture of recognition and accountability. By acknowledging and celebrating employees' contributions to security, organizations can strengthen their overall security posture and build a more proactive and engaged workforce. Regular security awareness campaigns are vital for maintaining a security-conscious culture within an organization. By providing consistent messaging, leveraging interactive tools and simulations, utilizing data analytics, and encouraging active participation, organizations can effectively enhance their employees' knowledge and readiness to handle cybersecurity threats. Incorporating coding examples and practical exercises into training materials further reinforces secure practices and helps employees apply their knowledge in real-world scenarios. Through ongoing campaigns and a commitment to continuous learning, organizations can build a resilient security culture and better protect against the evolving landscape of cyber threats.

Evaluating Training Effectiveness and Impact

Introduction

Evaluating the effectiveness and impact of cybersecurity training is crucial to ensuring that training programs meet their objectives and contribute to improving the organization's overall security posture. Effective evaluation involves measuring various aspects of the training program, including knowledge retention, behavior changes, and overall impact on security outcomes. This section outlines key methods and metrics for evaluating training effectiveness, providing insights into how organizations can assess and enhance their cybersecurity training efforts.

1. Assessing Knowledge Retention

1.1 Pre- and Post-Training Assessments

To gauge the effectiveness of training in improving employees' cybersecurity knowledge, pre- and post-training assessments are commonly used. Pre-training assessments establish a baseline of employees' existing knowledge, while post-training assessments measure the increase in knowledge following the training. These assessments can take the form of quizzes, tests, or practical exercises that cover key topics from the training program.

For example, a pre-training assessment might include questions about basic cybersecurity concepts, such as recognizing phishing emails or understanding secure password practices. A post-training assessment would then test the same concepts to evaluate how much employees have learned. The results can be analyzed to determine the effectiveness of the training and identify areas where additional focus may be needed.

1.2 Knowledge Retention over Time

Measuring knowledge retention over time helps assess whether employees continue to apply what they have learned in their daily work. Follow-up assessments conducted at regular intervals after the initial training can provide insights into how well employees retain and apply their knowledge. These assessments can include periodic quizzes, refresher courses, or scenario-based exercises that test employees' ability to recall and use cybersecurity principles.

For instance, a six-month follow-up assessment might revisit key topics from the training, such as identifying common cyber threats or implementing security best practices. Comparing the results of these assessments with the initial post-training assessments can help determine the long-term effectiveness of the training program.

2. Measuring Behavioral Changes

2.1 Tracking Incident Reporting Rates

One key indicator of the impact of cybersecurity training is the rate at which employees report potential security incidents. An increase in incident reporting rates following training can suggest that employees are more aware of potential threats and are actively applying their knowledge. Monitoring incident reporting rates can provide valuable insights into the effectiveness of the training program and highlight areas where further education may be needed.

For example, if the training program includes a module on recognizing phishing emails, an increase in the number of phishing attempts reported by employees could indicate that the training has successfully raised awareness about this threat.

2.2 Observing Changes in Security Practices

Behavioral changes in security practices can also be assessed through direct observations and self-reported data. Organizations can evaluate whether employees are following security best practices, such as using strong passwords, implementing multi-factor authentication, or adhering to data protection policies. This can be done through periodic security audits, reviews of security logs, or employee surveys.

For instance, a security audit might reveal an improvement in the use of strong passwords and secure authentication methods following a training program focused on password security. Surveys can also provide feedback on employees' adherence to security policies and their perceived confidence in handling security-related tasks.

3. Evaluating Overall Impact

3.1 Analyzing Security Incident Data

To assess the overall impact of cybersecurity training, organizations can analyze security incident data to determine whether there has been a reduction in the frequency or severity of incidents. By comparing incident data before and after the training program, organizations can evaluate whether the training has contributed to a decrease in security breaches or other negative outcomes.

For example, if the training program includes modules on detecting and responding to malware attacks, a reduction in malware incidents or successful mitigation of attacks following the training could indicate its effectiveness.

3.2 Gathering Employee Feedback

Employee feedback provides valuable insights into the perceived effectiveness and relevance of the training program. Surveys, interviews, and focus groups can be used to gather feedback on various aspects of the training, including content, delivery methods, and overall experience. Employees' perceptions of the training's usefulness and applicability can help identify strengths and areas for improvement.

For example, a post-training survey might ask employees to rate the clarity of the training content, the relevance of the scenarios, and their confidence in applying the knowledge. This feedback can inform future training improvements and ensure that the program continues to meet employees' needs.

4. Continuous Improvement and Adaptation

4.1 Incorporating Feedback into Training Updates

Continuous improvement of the training program is essential for maintaining its effectiveness and relevance. Feedback from assessments, incident data, and employee surveys should be used to make iterative improvements to the training content and delivery methods. This may involve updating training materials, incorporating new threat information, or adjusting the format to better engage employees.

For example, if feedback indicates that employees found certain topics confusing or challenging, the training program can be revised to provide clearer explanations or additional examples. Regular updates based on the latest cybersecurity trends and threats can also help ensure that the training remains current and effective.

4.2 Implementing Adaptive Learning Techniques

Adaptive learning techniques can enhance the effectiveness of cybersecurity training by tailoring the content and delivery to individual learners' needs. Adaptive learning platforms use data and analytics to customize the training experience based on employees' performance, learning preferences, and progress. This personalized approach helps address knowledge gaps and improve overall training outcomes.

For example, an adaptive learning system might provide additional resources or targeted exercises for employees who struggle with specific topics, while offering advanced content for those who demonstrate proficiency. By adapting the training to individual needs, organizations can ensure that employees receive the most relevant and effective instruction. Evaluating the effectiveness and impact of cybersecurity training is essential for ensuring that training programs achieve their intended goals and contribute to improving organizational security. By assessing knowledge retention, measuring behavioral changes, analyzing security incident data, and gathering employee feedback, organizations can gain valuable insights into the success of their training efforts. Continuous improvement and adaptation based on evaluation results help maintain the relevance and effectiveness of the training program, ultimately fostering a more secure and informed workforce.

Adapting Training for Different Roles and Skill Levels

In the realm of cybersecurity, a one-size-fits-all approach to training is often ineffective due to the diverse nature of job roles and varying levels of expertise within an organization. Adapting training programs to accommodate different roles and skill levels is crucial for ensuring that all employees receive relevant, actionable, and appropriately challenging instruction. This tailored approach helps maximize the effectiveness of training efforts and ensures that employees are equipped with the knowledge and skills necessary to handle their specific responsibilities securely. This section explores strategies for adapting cybersecurity training to different roles and skill levels, providing practical examples and considerations for effective implementation.

1. Tailoring Training Content to Job Roles

1.1 Role-Specific Training Modules

Cybersecurity training should be customized to address the specific responsibilities and risks associated with different job roles. Role-specific training modules ensure that employees receive content relevant to their day-to-day activities and the types of threats they are most likely to encounter. For example, a training module for IT staff might focus on advanced topics such as network security protocols, firewall configurations, and incident response strategies. Conversely, a training module for customer service representatives might emphasize recognizing phishing attempts, handling sensitive customer information, and secure communication practices.

Example:

- **IT Staff:** A module on network security might cover topics such as configuring VPNs, monitoring network traffic for unusual activity, and implementing intrusion detection systems. Practical exercises could include configuring firewall rules or analyzing network logs for signs of a potential breach.
- **Finance Department:** Training might include scenarios on detecting fraudulent transactions, securing financial data, and understanding regulatory compliance requirements. Exercises could involve identifying red flags in transaction data or responding to simulated data breaches.

1.2 Customizing Scenarios and Exercises

To enhance relevance, training scenarios and exercises should be tailored to reflect the specific challenges faced by different roles. Customizing scenarios allows employees to practice handling threats and situations that directly relate to their job functions. For example, a scenario for a system administrator might involve responding to a simulated ransomware attack on a company server, while a scenario for a marketing team might focus on securing social media accounts and identifying social engineering tactics.

Example:

- **System Administrators:** A scenario could simulate a ransomware attack where administrators must identify the attack vector, isolate affected systems, and implement recovery procedures. The exercise could include interactive elements such as decision points and real-time feedback.
- **HR Personnel:** A training scenario might involve handling a data breach involving employee personal information. HR staff could practice responding to the breach, notifying affected individuals, and implementing remediation measures.

2. Addressing Varying Skill Levels

2.1 Differentiated Learning Paths

Employees with different levels of cybersecurity knowledge and experience require differentiated learning paths to ensure they receive appropriate instruction. New employees or those with limited cybersecurity experience might benefit from foundational training that covers basic concepts and best practices. In contrast, experienced employees or those with specialized roles might require advanced training that delves into more complex topics and technical details.

Example:

- **Beginners:** A foundational training path might include introductory modules on cybersecurity basics, such as understanding common threats, secure password practices, and safe internet usage. Interactive quizzes and simple scenarios can reinforce these concepts.
- **Advanced Users:** An advanced learning path might include in-depth modules on topics such as threat hunting, advanced persistent threats (APTs), and incident management. This path could involve complex scenarios, hands-on labs, and detailed technical exercises.

2.2 Offering Progressive Training Levels

Progressive training levels allow employees to build upon their existing knowledge and skills over time. By offering a series of training levels, organizations can ensure that employees continue to develop their expertise and stay up-to-date with evolving threats. Progressive training can include basic, intermediate, and advanced levels, with each level building on the previous one.

Example:

- **Basic Level:** Covers fundamental concepts such as recognizing phishing emails, understanding data encryption, and following security policies. This level is suitable for employees new to cybersecurity or those requiring a refresher.
- **Intermediate Level:** Focuses on more advanced topics such as network security, vulnerability management, and secure software development practices. Employees with a basic understanding of cybersecurity can progress to this level to deepen their knowledge.
- **Advanced Level:** Delves into specialized areas such as threat intelligence, forensic analysis, and advanced malware analysis. This level is intended for employees with significant cybersecurity experience or those in technical roles.

3. Leveraging Technology for Personalized Training

3.1 Adaptive Learning Platforms

Adaptive learning platforms use data and analytics to tailor the training experience to individual learners' needs and skill levels. These platforms can adjust the content, difficulty, and pace of training based on employees' performance and progress. By providing personalized learning experiences, adaptive platforms ensure that employees receive instruction that matches their specific requirements and learning styles.

Example:

An adaptive learning platform might use algorithms to assess employees' responses to quizzes and scenarios, adjusting the difficulty of subsequent questions based on their performance. If an employee consistently answers questions correctly, the platform might present more challenging scenarios or advanced content. Conversely, if an employee struggles with certain topics, the platform can provide additional resources or remedial exercises to address knowledge gaps.

3.2 E-Learning Modules with Interactive Features

E-learning modules with interactive features, such as simulations, quizzes, and scenario-based exercises, enhance engagement and provide opportunities for hands-on practice. These modules can be customized to align with different roles and skill levels, offering relevant content and interactive elements that reinforce learning.

Example:

An e-learning module for cybersecurity might include interactive simulations where employees can practice responding to simulated attacks, such as a phishing email or a malware infection. The module might also include embedded quizzes that test employees' understanding of key concepts and provide immediate feedback.

4. Evaluating Training Outcomes

4.1 Monitoring Performance Metrics

Monitoring performance metrics, such as quiz scores, completion rates, and participation levels, helps assess the effectiveness of role-specific and skill-level training. Analyzing these metrics can provide insights into how well employees are grasping the content and whether additional support or adjustments are needed.

Example:

- **Quiz Scores:** Tracking quiz scores for different training modules can reveal which topics employees understand well and which areas may require further reinforcement. For instance, if employees consistently score lower on a module about secure coding practices, it may indicate a need for additional training or support in that area.
- **Participation Rates:** Monitoring participation rates in training modules can help assess engagement

levels and identify potential barriers to completion. Low participation rates might suggest the need for more engaging content or better communication about the importance of the training.

4.2 Gathering Feedback and Conducting Surveys

Collecting feedback from employees through surveys and interviews provides valuable insights into the effectiveness and relevance of the training. Feedback can highlight areas where training may need to be adjusted, such as content difficulty, clarity of instruction, or applicability to specific roles.

Example:

- **Surveys:** Post-training surveys can ask employees to rate their satisfaction with the training, the relevance of the content to their role, and their confidence in applying what they have learned. Survey results can inform future training improvements and help tailor content to better meet employees' needs.
- **Interviews:** Conducting interviews with employees can provide in-depth feedback on their training experience, including specific challenges they faced and suggestions for improvement. This qualitative feedback can complement quantitative metrics and

provide a more comprehensive view of training effectiveness.

Adapting cybersecurity training for different roles and skill levels is essential for ensuring that all employees receive relevant, engaging, and effective instruction. By tailoring training content to specific job functions, addressing varying levels of expertise, leveraging technology for personalized learning, and evaluating training outcomes, organizations can enhance the effectiveness of their training programs and better equip employees to handle cybersecurity challenges. A well-designed and customized training approach not only improves employees' knowledge and skills but also contributes to a more secure and resilient organizational environment.

Summary and Key Takeaways

Adapting cybersecurity training for different roles and skill levels is a critical component of an effective security awareness program. This approach ensures that all employees receive training that is relevant to their specific job functions and aligned with their existing knowledge and experience. By customizing training content, scenarios, and exercises to fit the diverse needs of various roles within the organization, companies can maximize the impact of their training efforts and enhance overall security posture.

Key Takeaways
1. **Role-Specific Training:** Tailoring training content to specific job roles ensures that employees receive relevant information and practical guidance related to their responsibilities. For instance, IT staff may need in-depth knowledge of network security, while customer service representatives might focus on recognizing phishing attempts. This targeted approach helps employees apply what they learn directly to their daily tasks.
2. **Customized Scenarios and Exercises:** Adapting training scenarios and exercises to reflect the challenges faced by different roles enhances engagement and learning outcomes. Role-specific scenarios allow employees to practice responding to threats and situations that are directly relevant to their job functions, making the training more applicable and effective.
3. **Differentiated Learning Paths:** Offering differentiated learning paths based on employees' skill levels ensures that training is appropriately challenging and educational. Beginners may start with foundational content, while advanced users can progress to more complex topics. This progressive

approach helps build and reinforce knowledge over time.

4. **Adaptive Learning Technologies:** Leveraging adaptive learning platforms and interactive e-learning modules allows for personalized training experiences that cater to individual needs and learning styles. These technologies can adjust content difficulty, pace, and format based on employees' performance, ensuring that they receive the most relevant and effective instruction.

5. **Monitoring and Evaluation:** Evaluating training effectiveness through performance metrics, feedback, and surveys provides valuable insights into how well the training is achieving its goals. Regular assessment of knowledge retention, behavioral changes, and overall impact helps identify areas for improvement and informs future training updates.

6. **Continuous Improvement:** Ongoing adaptation and enhancement of training programs based on evaluation results and employee feedback are essential for maintaining relevance and effectiveness. Incorporating new threat information, refining content, and addressing emerging needs

ensure that the training remains up-to-date and impactful.

By adopting these strategies, organizations can create a dynamic and responsive training program that effectively addresses the diverse needs of their workforce. This tailored approach not only improves employees' cybersecurity knowledge and skills but also strengthens the organization's overall security posture, making it better equipped to handle evolving cyber threats.

Chapter 4: Risk Management and Mitigation Strategies

4.1 Identifying Human-Centric Security Risks
4.2 Implementing Policies and Procedures to Mitigate Risks
4.3 The Role of User Behavior Analytics in Risk Management
4.4 Responding to Security Incidents: Roles and Responsibilities
4.5 Continuous Improvement and Risk Management Best Practices
4.6 Summary and Key Takeaways

Chapter 4: Risk Management and Mitigation Strategies

In the fast-evolving landscape of cybersecurity, managing and mitigating risk is essential to safeguarding sensitive data and maintaining the integrity of systems. Effective risk management strategies begin with identifying potential threats and vulnerabilities, assessing the impact of these risks, and prioritizing them based on their severity. The goal is not only to mitigate existing risks but also to anticipate future threats.

A comprehensive risk management framework typically follows a cyclical process: risk identification, risk assessment, risk mitigation, and continuous monitoring. During the identification phase, organizations must understand their assets, the value they hold, and the specific threats they face. The assessment phase involves analyzing the likelihood and impact of these risks, often using quantitative or qualitative approaches. The focus then shifts to mitigation strategies, where proactive steps are taken to reduce risks to acceptable levels. These strategies may include implementing firewalls, encryption, multi-factor authentication, or more advanced AI-driven solutions that continuously monitor for anomalies and potential breaches.

Beyond technical controls, fostering a culture of cybersecurity awareness is a key component of risk mitigation. Regular training programs for employees, developing incident response protocols, and enforcing policies for data handling all contribute to reducing human-related risks, which are often the weakest link in an organization's defense.

Finally, continuous monitoring is vital. As new vulnerabilities emerge, businesses must remain agile, updating their risk management strategies to adapt to evolving threats. In an increasingly interconnected world, managing cybersecurity risks is not a one-time task but an ongoing effort that requires vigilance, adaptation, and collaboration across all levels of an organization.

Introduction

Risk management and mitigation are central to maintaining robust cybersecurity defenses and ensuring organizational resilience against potential threats. This chapter explores the key concepts and strategies associated with managing and mitigating cybersecurity risks, offering practical insights and techniques for implementing effective risk management practices. By understanding and applying these strategies, organizations can better identify, assess, and address cybersecurity risks, minimizing their impact and enhancing overall security posture.

1. Understanding Cybersecurity Risk

1.1 Definition and Scope of Cybersecurity Risk

Cybersecurity risk refers to the potential for loss or harm resulting from threats to information systems and data. This includes risks associated with unauthorized access, data breaches, malware attacks, and other cyber threats. Understanding the scope of cybersecurity risk involves recognizing the various types of threats, vulnerabilities, and potential impacts on an organization's assets, operations, and reputation.

Example:

A financial institution might face risks from data breaches that could expose sensitive customer information, leading to financial losses and reputational damage. Understanding the scope of these risks involves identifying potential attack vectors, such as phishing or insider threats, and evaluating the potential impact on the organization's operations and customer trust.

1.2 Risk Assessment Frameworks

Risk assessment frameworks provide structured approaches for identifying, analyzing, and prioritizing cybersecurity risks. These frameworks help organizations systematically evaluate potential threats and vulnerabilities, determine their likelihood and impact, and develop appropriate mitigation strategies.

Example:

- **NIST Risk Management Framework (RMF):** Provides a structured approach for managing risk through a series of steps, including risk assessment, risk mitigation, and ongoing monitoring. The framework emphasizes a continuous cycle of risk management to adapt to changing threat landscapes.
- **ISO/IEC 27005:** Offers guidelines for information security risk management, focusing on the risk assessment process, risk treatment options, and the need for ongoing risk monitoring and review.

2. Risk Identification and Analysis

2.1 Identifying Threats and Vulnerabilities

Effective risk management begins with identifying potential threats and vulnerabilities within an organization's information systems. Threats may include external attacks, such as cybercriminal activities, as well as internal risks, such as employee misconduct or accidental data loss. Vulnerabilities are weaknesses in systems or processes that can be exploited by threats.

Example:

- **Threats:** Cybercriminals targeting an organization's network with ransomware, or insider threats from employees with malicious intent.
- **Vulnerabilities:** Outdated software with known security flaws, unpatched systems, or weak password policies.

2.2 Conducting Risk Assessments

Risk assessments involve evaluating the likelihood and potential impact of identified threats and vulnerabilities. This process typically includes qualitative and quantitative methods to assess risk levels and prioritize mitigation efforts.

Example:

- **Qualitative Risk Assessment:** Uses subjective methods to assess the likelihood and impact of risks, often through expert judgment and risk matrices. For example, assessing the risk of a data breach as "high," "medium," or "low" based on the potential impact on the organization.
- **Quantitative Risk Assessment:** Employs numerical methods to calculate risk levels, often using statistical data and models. For instance, calculating the potential financial loss from a cyber

attack based on historical data and potential attack vectors.

3. Risk Mitigation Strategies

3.1 Implementing Technical Controls

Technical controls are security measures designed to protect information systems from cyber threats. These controls include technologies and practices such as firewalls, intrusion detection systems, encryption, and secure authentication methods.

Example:

- **Firewalls:** Act as barriers between internal networks and external threats, filtering incoming and outgoing traffic based on predefined security rules.
- **Encryption:** Protects data by converting it into a format that is unreadable without the appropriate decryption key, ensuring data confidentiality during transmission and storage.

3.2 Developing Policies and Procedures

Establishing comprehensive cybersecurity policies and procedures helps guide organizational practices and ensure consistent risk management. These policies should cover areas such as data protection, incident response, access control, and employee training.

Example:
- **Data Protection Policy:** Outlines procedures for handling and securing sensitive information, including data classification, access controls, and data retention practices.
- **Incident Response Plan:** Provides a structured approach for responding to and managing cybersecurity incidents, including roles and responsibilities, communication protocols, and recovery procedures.

3.3 Enhancing Employee Awareness and Training

Employees play a crucial role in mitigating cybersecurity risks through their awareness and adherence to security practices. Ongoing training and awareness programs help employees recognize and respond to potential threats, reducing the risk of human error.

Example:
- **Phishing Awareness Training:** Educates employees on recognizing phishing attempts and avoiding malicious links or attachments. Training may include interactive simulations and real-life scenarios to reinforce learning.
- **Secure Practices Training:** Provides guidance on secure practices, such as creating strong passwords,

using multi-factor authentication, and protecting sensitive data.

4. Risk Monitoring and Review

4.1 Continuous Monitoring

Continuous monitoring involves the ongoing observation and analysis of an organization's information systems to detect and respond to security threats in real-time. This includes the use of monitoring tools, such as Security Information and Event Management (SIEM) systems, to track system activities, identify anomalies, and respond to potential incidents.

Example:

- **SIEM Systems:** Aggregate and analyze security event data from various sources, providing real-time alerts and insights into potential threats. SIEM systems can help detect unusual activities, such as unauthorized access attempts or abnormal network traffic.

4.2 Regular Risk Reviews and Updates

Regular reviews and updates of risk management practices are essential for adapting to evolving threats and changing organizational needs. Risk reviews should be conducted periodically to assess the effectiveness of existing controls, identify new risks, and update mitigation strategies as necessary.

Example:

- **Annual Risk Reviews:** Evaluate the effectiveness of risk management practices and identify areas for improvement. Reviews may include updating risk assessments, revising policies, and incorporating new threat intelligence.
- **Control Testing:** Periodically test the effectiveness of security controls through activities such as penetration testing, vulnerability assessments, and security audits.

Effective risk management and mitigation strategies are vital for safeguarding an organization's information systems and data from cybersecurity threats. By understanding and applying key concepts such as risk identification, assessment, and mitigation, organizations can develop robust defenses and enhance their overall security posture. Implementing technical controls, developing comprehensive policies, and fostering employee awareness contribute to a resilient cybersecurity framework. Continuous monitoring and regular risk reviews ensure that risk management practices remain effective and responsive to evolving threats. Through these strategies, organizations can better protect their assets, maintain operational integrity, and achieve long-term security resilience.

4.1 Identifying Human-Centric Security Risks

Human-centric security risks stem from the interplay between human behavior and cybersecurity. These risks are often associated with the actions, decisions, and interactions of individuals within an organization, and they can significantly impact the overall security posture. Identifying these risks requires an understanding of how human factors contribute to vulnerabilities and potential threats. This section delves into the identification of human-centric security risks, exploring common behaviors and scenarios that pose risks, and offering strategies to recognize and address these vulnerabilities.

1. Understanding Human-Centric Risks

1.1 Definition and Scope

Human-centric security risks refer to vulnerabilities and threats that arise from human actions, behaviors, and decisions. These risks can be intentional, such as malicious insider threats, or unintentional, such as mistakes or negligence. Understanding these risks involves recognizing how human behavior interacts with security policies, systems, and practices, and identifying the specific areas where these interactions can lead to security breaches or incidents.

Example:
- **Intentional Risks:** Employees deliberately compromising security for personal gain or malicious intent, such as stealing sensitive information or sabotaging systems.
- **Unintentional Risks:** Accidental actions that lead to security breaches, such as falling for phishing scams, mishandling sensitive data, or failing to follow security protocols.

1.2 Key Human-Centric Risk Factors

Several key factors contribute to human-centric security risks:

- **Lack of Awareness:** Employees may not be aware of security best practices, leading to risky behaviors such as weak password usage or clicking on malicious links.
- **Poor Training:** Inadequate or ineffective security training can result in employees not recognizing or responding appropriately to security threats.
- **Behavioral Habits:** Certain behavioral tendencies, such as complacency or overconfidence, can lead to

risky actions or negligence in following security protocols.
- **Social Engineering:** Attackers exploit human psychology through tactics like phishing, pretexting, and baiting to manipulate individuals into divulging sensitive information or performing actions that compromise security.

2. Common Human-Centric Risks

2.1 Phishing and Social Engineering

Phishing and social engineering attacks exploit human psychology to deceive individuals into revealing confidential information or performing actions that compromise security. These attacks often involve deceptive communications, such as emails or phone calls, that appear legitimate but are designed to trick individuals into providing sensitive data or credentials.

Example:

- **Phishing Emails:** An attacker sends an email that appears to be from a trusted source, such as a bank or company executive, asking the recipient to click on a link or provide login credentials. If the recipient falls for the scam, their credentials may be stolen, leading to unauthorized access to systems or data.

2.2 Insider Threats

Insider threats involve individuals within an organization who misuse their access to information systems or data for malicious purposes. These threats can come from employees, contractors, or other insiders who intentionally or unintentionally cause harm to the organization.

Example:

- **Malicious Insiders:** An employee with access to sensitive data intentionally leaks information to competitors or engages in fraudulent activities. This type of insider threat can result in significant financial and reputational damage.

2.3 Human Error

Human error is a common source of security incidents, often resulting from mistakes or negligence. Errors can occur during routine tasks, such as handling data or configuring systems, and may lead to vulnerabilities or breaches.

Example:

- **Misconfigured Systems:** An administrator accidentally misconfigures a firewall or exposes sensitive data through improper settings, creating a vulnerability that can be exploited by attackers.

2.4 Password and Authentication Issues

Weak or poorly managed passwords and authentication practices contribute to human-centric security risks. Common issues include the use of easily guessable passwords, password reuse, and inadequate multi-factor authentication (MFA).

Example:

- **Weak Passwords:** Employees use simple, easily guessable passwords for multiple accounts, making it easier for attackers to gain unauthorized access. For example, using "password123" or "admin" as a password increases the risk of a successful attack.

3. Identifying Human-Centric Risks in Practice

3.1 Conducting Risk Assessments

Risk assessments help identify and evaluate human-centric security risks by analyzing potential vulnerabilities and threats associated with employee behavior and practices. This process involves reviewing security incidents, analyzing patterns of behavior, and assessing the effectiveness of existing controls.

Example:

- **Incident Analysis:** Reviewing past security incidents to identify common patterns of human error or risky behavior. For instance, if multiple incidents involve phishing emails, it may indicate a need for improved training and awareness.

3.2 Performing Vulnerability Assessments

Vulnerability assessments focus on identifying weaknesses in systems and processes that could be exploited due to human actions. This includes evaluating the effectiveness of security measures and identifying areas where human behavior contributes to vulnerabilities.

Example:

- **Penetration Testing:** Conducting simulated attacks to assess how employees respond to security threats and identifying areas where human error may lead to vulnerabilities. For example, testing how employees handle phishing attempts or respond to social engineering tactics.

3.3 Implementing Behavioral Analytics

Behavioral analytics tools analyze user behavior patterns to detect anomalies and potential risks. These tools use data from various sources, such as login patterns and access logs, to identify unusual or risky behavior that may indicate a security threat.

Example:

- **Anomaly Detection:** Monitoring user behavior for signs of abnormal activity, such as accessing sensitive data outside of normal work hours or from unfamiliar locations. Behavioral analytics can help identify potential insider threats or compromised accounts.

4. Mitigating Human-Centric Risks

4.1 Enhancing Awareness and Training Programs

Comprehensive training programs and awareness initiatives are essential for mitigating human-centric risks. These programs should educate employees about common threats, secure practices, and the importance of following security policies.

Example:

- **Phishing Simulation Training:** Conducting regular phishing simulations to help employees recognize and respond to phishing attempts. Simulations can include mock emails and interactive exercises that test employees' ability to identify suspicious communications.

4.2 Developing Strong Security Policies

Establishing and enforcing clear security policies helps guide employee behavior and reduce the likelihood of risky actions. Policies should cover areas such as password management, data handling, and incident reporting.

Example:

- **Password Policy:** Implementing a strong password policy that requires employees to use complex passwords, change them regularly, and avoid password reuse. The policy should also mandate the use of multi-factor authentication for critical systems.

4.3 Fostering a Security-Conscious Culture

Building a security-conscious culture involves promoting awareness and accountability among employees. This includes encouraging open communication about security concerns, recognizing and addressing risky behaviors, and creating an environment where security is prioritized.

Example:

- **Security Champions:** Designating security champions within departments to promote best practices, provide guidance, and act as a resource for employees. Security champions can help reinforce security policies and provide support for addressing potential risks.

Identifying human-centric security risks is a crucial aspect of effective cybersecurity risk management. By understanding the nature of human-centric risks, recognizing common sources of vulnerability, and implementing targeted strategies for mitigation, organizations can better protect themselves against the threats posed by human behavior. Enhanced awareness, comprehensive training, strong policies, and a security-conscious culture are key components in addressing human-centric risks and improving overall security resilience. Through these efforts, organizations can reduce the impact of human-related vulnerabilities and strengthen their overall cybersecurity posture.

4.2 Implementing Policies and Procedures to Mitigate Risks

Implementing effective policies and procedures is fundamental to mitigating cybersecurity risks and establishing a robust defense against potential threats. These policies and procedures provide a structured framework for managing security practices, guiding employee behavior, and ensuring consistent application of security measures across the organization. This section explores the critical aspects of developing, implementing, and maintaining cybersecurity policies and procedures, offering practical insights and recommendations for effective risk management.

1. Developing Cybersecurity Policies

1.1 Establishing Policy Objectives

The first step in developing cybersecurity policies is to define clear objectives that align with the organization's overall security goals. These objectives should address key areas of risk, including data protection, access control, incident response, and compliance with regulatory requirements. Establishing clear policy objectives helps ensure that policies are focused, relevant, and capable of effectively mitigating identified risks.

Example:
- **Data Protection Policy:** Aims to safeguard sensitive information by specifying procedures for data classification, handling, encryption, and storage. Objectives might include preventing unauthorized access, ensuring data integrity, and complying with data protection regulations.

1.2 Drafting Comprehensive Policies

Comprehensive cybersecurity policies should cover various aspects of security and provide detailed guidelines for employees and management. Key elements of effective policies include:
- **Scope and Applicability:** Clearly define the scope of the policy and identify who it applies to, including employees, contractors, and third-party vendors.

- **Roles and Responsibilities:** Outline the roles and responsibilities of individuals and teams involved in implementing and adhering to the policy. This includes defining responsibilities for data protection, incident reporting, and policy enforcement.
- **Procedures and Guidelines:** Provide detailed procedures and guidelines for specific security practices, such as password management, data access, and incident response. This includes specifying steps for compliance and enforcement.
- **Compliance Requirements:** Address any legal, regulatory, or industry-specific compliance requirements that the policy must meet, ensuring alignment with relevant standards and regulations.

Example:
- **Access Control Policy:** Defines guidelines for granting and managing access to systems and data, including user authentication, authorization processes, and periodic reviews of access rights. The policy should also outline procedures for revoking access when employees leave the organization or change roles.

1.3 Reviewing and Approving Policies

Once drafted, cybersecurity policies should be reviewed and approved by relevant stakeholders, including senior management, legal advisors, and IT security professionals. This review process ensures that policies are comprehensive, aligned with organizational objectives, and legally compliant. Regular reviews and updates are also necessary to keep policies current with evolving threats and changes in regulatory requirements.

Example:

- **Policy Review Committee:** A committee comprising representatives from IT, legal, compliance, and other relevant departments reviews the policy to ensure it meets organizational needs and regulatory requirements. The committee may recommend revisions or updates based on feedback and changes in the threat landscape.

2. Implementing Security Procedures

2.1 Communicating Policies and Procedures

Effective communication is crucial for ensuring that employees understand and adhere to cybersecurity policies and procedures. Organizations should use various communication channels, such as email, intranet, and training sessions, to disseminate information about policies and procedures.

Example:
- **Policy Awareness Campaign:** Launch a campaign to inform employees about new or updated policies, using email announcements, posters, and intranet updates. The campaign should highlight key policy elements and provide resources for further information.

2.2 Training and Education

Training and education are essential for ensuring that employees understand the policies and procedures and can apply them effectively. Training programs should cover the content of the policies, practical implementation, and the importance of adhering to security practices.

Example:
- **Mandatory Security Training:** Require all employees to complete training on cybersecurity policies, including interactive modules and quizzes to reinforce understanding. Training should address specific procedures, such as secure password creation and data handling practices.

2.3 Integrating Policies into Daily Operations

Integrating cybersecurity policies into daily operations involves incorporating security practices into routine processes and workflows. This includes embedding security controls into systems, automating compliance checks, and ensuring that policies are part of everyday tasks.

Example:

- **Automated Access Controls:** Implement automated systems for managing user access, such as role-based access control (RBAC) and multi-factor authentication (MFA). These systems help enforce access control policies and reduce the risk of unauthorized access.

3. Monitoring and Enforcement

3.1 Monitoring Policy Compliance

Monitoring is essential for ensuring that policies and procedures are being followed and identifying potential areas of non-compliance. This involves implementing monitoring tools and conducting regular audits to assess adherence to security practices.

Example:

- **Compliance Audits:** Conduct periodic audits to evaluate compliance with cybersecurity policies and procedures. Audits should review access logs, security configurations, and incident reports to ensure that policies are being effectively implemented.

3.2 Enforcement and Discipline

Enforcement measures ensure that employees adhere to cybersecurity policies and address any violations or non-compliance. Organizations should establish clear procedures for reporting and investigating policy breaches and define appropriate disciplinary actions.

Example:

- **Incident Reporting Mechanism:** Provide a formal process for employees to report suspected policy violations or security incidents. This mechanism should include guidelines for reporting, investigating, and addressing breaches, along with potential disciplinary actions.

4. Reviewing and Updating Policies

4.1 Periodic Policy Reviews

Regular reviews and updates of cybersecurity policies are necessary to keep them relevant and effective. Reviews should consider changes in the threat landscape, technological advancements, and updates to regulatory requirements.

Example:

- **Annual Policy Review:** Schedule annual reviews of cybersecurity policies to assess their effectiveness and relevance. The review process should involve input from stakeholders and updates based on recent developments in cybersecurity and compliance.

4.2 Adapting to Changes

Policies should be adapted to address emerging threats and changes in the organization's environment. This includes updating policies in response to new vulnerabilities, regulatory changes, or changes in organizational structure or technology.

Example:

- **Policy Update Process:** Implement a process for updating policies to address new risks or regulatory requirements. This process should include reviewing and revising policies, communicating updates to employees, and providing additional training as needed.

Implementing effective policies and procedures is crucial for mitigating cybersecurity risks and ensuring that an organization maintains a strong security posture. By developing comprehensive policies, communicating and training employees, integrating security practices into daily operations, and monitoring and enforcing compliance, organizations can manage risks effectively and protect their assets. Regular reviews and updates ensure that policies remain relevant and effective in addressing evolving threats and changing organizational needs. Through these efforts, organizations can enhance their overall cybersecurity resilience and reduce the impact of potential risks.

4.3 The Role of User Behavior Analytics in Risk Management

Introduction

User Behavior Analytics (UBA) plays a critical role in modern cybersecurity risk management by providing insights into the patterns and anomalies in user activities that could indicate potential threats. By leveraging advanced analytical techniques and technologies, UBA helps organizations detect, assess, and mitigate risks associated with user behavior. This section explores the role of UBA in risk management, including its key components, methodologies, and practical applications in identifying and addressing security risks.

1. Understanding User Behavior Analytics

1.1 Definition and Scope

User Behavior Analytics (UBA) involves the collection, analysis, and interpretation of data related to user activities within an organization's IT environment. UBA focuses on understanding normal user behavior and identifying deviations that may signal malicious activity, insider threats, or other security risks. By analyzing patterns such as login behavior, file access, and network interactions, UBA helps organizations detect unusual or suspicious activities that may require further investigation.

Example:

- **Normal Behavior Patterns:** Typical user activities include regular logins during business hours, accessing files relevant to their job role, and communicating with colleagues. UBA establishes baselines for these activities to identify deviations.

1.2 Components of UBA

UBA systems typically consist of several key components:

- **Data Collection:** Aggregates data from various sources, including login logs, network traffic, application usage, and file access.
- **Behavioral Analysis:** Applies statistical and machine learning techniques to analyze user behavior and identify patterns or anomalies.
- **Alerting and Reporting:** Generates alerts and reports based on detected anomalies or deviations from established baselines.
- **Investigation and Response:** Provides tools and processes for investigating potential security incidents and responding to identified threats.

Example:

- **Data Collection Tools:** Tools that collect data from user activities, such as Security Information and Event Management (SIEM) systems and user activity monitoring (UAM) solutions.

2. Implementing UBA in Risk Management

2.1 Establishing Baselines for Normal Behavior

To effectively use UBA, organizations must first establish baselines for normal user behavior. This involves analyzing historical data to identify typical patterns of activity and create profiles for different user roles and functions. Baselines help differentiate between normal fluctuations and genuine security threats.

Example:

- **Baseline Creation:** Analyze historical login times, file access patterns, and network usage for different user roles to create a profile of normal behavior. This profile serves as a reference for detecting anomalies.

2.2 Detecting Anomalies and Potential Threats

UBA systems use advanced algorithms and machine learning techniques to detect anomalies and potential threats based on deviations from established baselines. Anomalies may include unusual login times, access to sensitive files, or atypical network activity. Detection capabilities can help identify potential insider threats, compromised accounts, or malicious activities.

Example:

- **Anomaly Detection:** An employee logging in from an unusual geographic location or accessing files they do not normally interact with may trigger an alert for further investigation.

2.3 Integrating UBA with Other Security Measures

UBA should be integrated with other security measures, such as SIEM systems, intrusion detection systems (IDS), and endpoint protection solutions. Integration allows for a more comprehensive approach to risk management, combining behavioral insights with traditional security controls to enhance threat detection and response.

Example:

- **SIEM Integration:** UBA data can be fed into a SIEM system to correlate user behavior anomalies with other security events, providing a more complete view of potential threats.

3. Benefits of User Behavior Analytics

3.1 Improved Threat Detection

UBA enhances threat detection by focusing on user behavior patterns and identifying deviations that may indicate security risks. This approach helps detect sophisticated threats that may evade traditional security measures, such as insider threats and compromised accounts.

Example:

- **Insider Threat Detection:** UBA can identify patterns indicative of insider threats, such as an employee accessing sensitive data outside of their normal job functions or exhibiting unusual behavior.

3.2 Reduced False Positives

By analyzing user behavior within the context of established baselines, UBA reduces the number of false positives compared to traditional security alerts. Accurate detection of genuine threats helps minimize disruptions and ensures that security teams can focus on real issues.

Example:

- **False Positive Reduction:** Anomalies detected by UBA, such as a sudden increase in file downloads, are assessed in the context of normal user behavior to determine if they represent a legitimate threat or a false alarm.

3.3 Enhanced Incident Response

UBA provides valuable insights that support effective incident response. By understanding user behavior patterns and identifying anomalies, security teams can prioritize investigations, respond to incidents more effectively, and mitigate potential impacts.

Example:

- **Incident Prioritization:** UBA alerts help security teams prioritize incidents based on the severity and potential impact of the detected anomalies, allowing for a more targeted response.

4. Challenges and Considerations

4.1 Privacy and Data Protection

Implementing UBA requires careful consideration of privacy and data protection concerns. Organizations must ensure that user behavior data is collected and analyzed in compliance with relevant regulations and privacy policies, and that data is handled securely.

Example:

- **Data Privacy Compliance:** Implementing data protection measures, such as anonymizing user data and adhering to privacy regulations (e.g., GDPR, CCPA), to ensure that UBA practices do not infringe on user privacy.

4.2 Complexity and Resource Requirements

UBA systems can be complex and resource-intensive, requiring significant investment in technology and expertise. Organizations must balance the benefits of UBA with the associated costs and ensure that the system is effectively integrated into their existing security infrastructure.

Example:

- **Resource Allocation:** Allocating resources for UBA implementation, including hardware, software, and skilled personnel, and ensuring that the system is properly integrated with other security measures.

5. Best Practices for UBA Implementation

5.1 Define Clear Objectives

Clearly define the objectives of implementing UBA, including the specific risks to be addressed and the expected outcomes. This helps ensure that UBA efforts are aligned with organizational goals and risk management strategies.

Example:

- **Objective Setting:** Establish objectives such as improving insider threat detection or enhancing the accuracy of threat alerts to guide the implementation and use of UBA.

5.2 Regularly Update Baselines

Regularly update baselines for normal behavior to account for changes in user roles, organizational structure, and business processes. This helps maintain the accuracy and relevance of UBA systems.

Example:
- **Baseline Updates:** Periodically review and update baseline profiles to reflect changes in user behavior, such as new job functions or shifts in work patterns.

5.3 Integrate with Existing Security Frameworks

Integrate UBA with existing security frameworks and tools to enhance overall risk management. Ensure that UBA data is used in conjunction with other security measures to provide a comprehensive view of potential threats.

Example:
- **Integration Strategy:** Develop a strategy for integrating UBA with SIEM systems, IDS, and other security tools to create a unified approach to threat detection and response.

User Behavior Analytics (UBA) is a powerful tool in risk management, providing valuable insights into user activities and identifying potential threats based on deviations from established behavior patterns. By implementing UBA effectively, organizations can enhance threat detection, reduce false positives, and improve incident response. However, it is essential to address challenges such as privacy concerns and resource requirements, and to follow best practices for successful implementation. With a well-integrated UBA system, organizations can strengthen their security posture and better manage risks associated with user behavior.

4.4 Responding to Security Incidents: Roles and Responsibilities

Effective response to security incidents is crucial for minimizing damage, ensuring business continuity, and protecting organizational assets. A well-defined incident response plan that clearly outlines roles and responsibilities is essential for a coordinated and efficient response. This section delves into the key roles and responsibilities involved in responding to security incidents, including the formation of an incident response team, the responsibilities of various stakeholders, and the coordination of actions during an incident.

1. Forming an Incident Response Team

1.1 Composition of the Incident Response Team

The Incident Response Team (IRT) is a specialized group responsible for managing and responding to security incidents. The composition of the team typically includes representatives from various departments, each bringing specific expertise to the response process. Common roles within the IRT include:

- **Incident Response Manager:** Oversees the overall incident response process, coordinates the efforts of the team, and communicates with senior management.
- **Security Analysts:** Analyze and investigate security incidents, identify the nature and scope of the threat, and implement technical measures to contain and mitigate the impact.
- **IT Support:** Provides technical assistance, including system restorations, network reconfigurations, and data recovery.
- **Legal and Compliance Representatives:** Ensure that the response complies with legal and regulatory requirements, and handle any legal implications of the incident.
- **Communication Specialist:** Manages internal and external communication, including notifying stakeholders, customers, and the media as appropriate.

Example:
- **Incident Response Manager:** A dedicated individual responsible for overseeing all aspects of

the incident response, from initial detection to final resolution, ensuring that the team follows established protocols and maintains effective communication with all stakeholders.

1.2 Responsibilities of Team Members

Each member of the IRT has specific responsibilities that contribute to the overall response effort:

- **Incident Response Manager:** Coordinates the response, allocates resources, and provides regular updates to senior management. Ensures that the incident response plan is followed and that all team members perform their designated tasks.
- **Security Analysts:** Conduct forensic analysis, identify the root cause of the incident, and implement containment and remediation measures. They also gather and preserve evidence for potential legal action or regulatory reporting.
- **IT Support:** Assists in the technical aspects of the response, such as isolating affected systems, restoring services, and applying patches or fixes. Supports the security analysts in addressing vulnerabilities and recovering data.
- **Legal and Compliance Representatives:** Review the incident response activities for legal and

regulatory compliance, handle reporting requirements, and manage any potential legal consequences.

- **Communication Specialist:** Develops and disseminates communication materials, manages media inquiries, and ensures consistent messaging to all stakeholders. Coordinates with the incident response manager to provide accurate and timely information.

2. Incident Response Phases

2.1 Preparation

Preparation involves establishing and maintaining the incident response capabilities and readiness. This includes developing an incident response plan, setting up communication protocols, conducting training and simulations, and ensuring that the necessary tools and resources are available.

Example:

- **Incident Response Plan:** A documented plan that outlines the procedures for detecting, responding to, and recovering from security incidents. Includes contact information for team members, detailed response procedures, and escalation paths.

2.2 Detection and Identification

Detection and identification involve recognizing and confirming the occurrence of a security incident. This phase requires monitoring systems for signs of incidents, analyzing alerts, and validating the nature and scope of the threat.

Example:

- **Alert Analysis:** Security analysts review alerts generated by monitoring systems, such as intrusion detection systems (IDS) or security information and event management (SIEM) systems, to determine whether they indicate a genuine security incident.

2.3 Containment

Containment aims to limit the spread of the incident and prevent further damage. This phase includes both short-term and long-term containment measures, such as isolating affected systems, blocking malicious traffic, and disabling compromised accounts.

Example:

- **Short-Term Containment:** Immediate actions taken to isolate affected systems, such as disconnecting them from the network or shutting them down, to prevent the spread of the incident.
- **Long-Term Containment:** Implementing measures to secure the environment while a more

comprehensive remediation plan is developed, such as applying temporary security controls or restricting access.

2.4 Eradication

Eradication involves removing the root cause of the incident and ensuring that all traces of the threat are eliminated from the affected systems. This phase includes activities such as removing malware, closing vulnerabilities, and applying patches or updates.

Example:

- **Malware Removal:** Security analysts identify and remove malicious software from infected systems, using tools such as antivirus scanners or specialized malware removal utilities.

2.5 Recovery

Recovery focuses on restoring normal operations and services while ensuring that the threat has been fully addressed. This phase includes restoring systems from backups, verifying system integrity, and monitoring for any signs of residual or recurring issues.

Example:

- **System Restoration:** IT support restores affected systems from clean backups, verifies that systems are functioning correctly, and ensures that all necessary security patches have been applied.

2.6 Lessons Learned

The lessons learned phase involves reviewing the incident response process to identify strengths, weaknesses, and areas for improvement. This phase includes conducting a post-incident review, documenting findings, and updating the incident response plan based on the insights gained.

Example:

- **Post-Incident Review:** A meeting conducted after the resolution of the incident to evaluate the response process, discuss what worked well and what could be improved, and update procedures accordingly.

3. Communication and Coordination

3.1 Internal Communication

Effective internal communication ensures that all relevant parties are informed of the incident status and response efforts. The incident response manager coordinates with various departments to provide updates and ensure that everyone is aligned with the response strategy.

Example:

- **Internal Briefings:** Regular updates provided to senior management, department heads, and other stakeholders about the incident's status, impact, and response actions.

3.2 External Communication

External communication involves managing interactions with external stakeholders, including customers, partners, regulators, and the media. The communication specialist is responsible for crafting and delivering messages that accurately convey the situation and the organization's response.

Example:

- **Customer Notifications:** Informing customers about the incident, its impact on services, and any actions they need to take, such as changing passwords or monitoring account activity.

4. Training and Preparedness

4.1 Regular Training

Regular training is essential for ensuring that incident response team members are familiar with their roles and responsibilities and can effectively execute the incident response plan. Training should include simulations and tabletop exercises to practice responding to various types of incidents.

Example:

- **Tabletop Exercises:** Simulated incident scenarios that involve the entire incident response team, allowing members to practice their roles and coordinate their actions in a controlled environment.

4.2 Updating the Response Plan

The incident response plan should be reviewed and updated regularly based on lessons learned from previous incidents, changes in the threat landscape, and evolving organizational needs. Ensuring that the plan remains current and relevant is critical for maintaining an effective response capability.

Example:

- **Plan Review and Revision:** Periodic review of the incident response plan to incorporate feedback from training exercises, new threats, and changes in organizational structure or technology.

Responding to security incidents effectively requires a well-defined incident response plan, a skilled and coordinated incident response team, and clear roles and responsibilities for all stakeholders. By following established procedures, communicating effectively, and maintaining preparedness through training and plan updates, organizations can manage incidents efficiently, minimize damage, and enhance their overall security posture. A proactive approach to incident response not only helps address immediate threats but also strengthens the organization's ability to handle future challenges.

4.5 Continuous Improvement and Risk Management Best Practices

Continuous improvement and the application of best practices are essential components of effective risk management in cybersecurity. As the threat landscape evolves, organizations must adapt their strategies to address emerging risks and enhance their overall security posture. This section explores the principles of continuous improvement in risk management and outlines best practices that organizations can adopt to maintain robust security defenses and respond effectively to new challenges.

1. Embracing Continuous Improvement

1.1 The Concept of Continuous Improvement

Continuous improvement is a proactive approach to enhancing organizational processes, practices, and technologies over time. In the context of cybersecurity risk management, this involves regularly assessing and refining risk management strategies, incident response protocols, and security controls to address emerging threats and vulnerabilities. Continuous improvement ensures that an organization's security measures remain effective and relevant in a constantly changing environment.

Example:

- **Regular Audits:** Conducting periodic security audits to evaluate the effectiveness of existing controls and identify areas for enhancement. Audits provide valuable insights into potential weaknesses and opportunities for improvement.

1.2 Feedback Loops and Iterative Enhancements

Incorporating feedback loops into risk management processes allows organizations to gather insights from various sources, including incident post-mortems, security assessments, and user feedback. This feedback is used to drive iterative enhancements, ensuring that security measures evolve based on real-world experiences and emerging threats.

Example:

- **Incident Post-Mortem Reviews:** After an incident, reviewing the response process, identifying lessons learned, and updating policies and procedures accordingly. This iterative approach helps refine response strategies and improve overall security posture.

2. Risk Management Best Practices

2.1 Establishing a Risk Management Framework

A well-defined risk management framework provides a structured approach to identifying, assessing, and mitigating risks. Frameworks such as the NIST Cybersecurity Framework, ISO/IEC 27001, and the FAIR (Factor Analysis of Information Risk) model offer guidelines for managing risks in a systematic and consistent manner.

Example:

- **NIST Cybersecurity Framework:** A comprehensive framework that includes standards, guidelines, and best practices for managing cybersecurity risks. It provides a structured approach to identifying and addressing risks across various domains.

2.2 Implementing Layered Security Controls

Layered security, or defense-in-depth, involves deploying multiple layers of security controls to protect against threats. This approach reduces the likelihood of a single point of failure and enhances the organization's ability to detect, prevent, and respond to attacks.

Example:

- **Multi-Layered Security:** Combining firewalls, intrusion detection systems (IDS), antivirus software, encryption, and access controls to create a multi-layered defense that addresses different aspects of security.

2.3 Conducting Regular Risk Assessments

Regular risk assessments help organizations identify potential vulnerabilities and evaluate the effectiveness of existing controls. Assessments should be conducted periodically and following significant changes to the IT environment, such as new system deployments or changes in business processes.

Example:

- **Vulnerability Scanning:** Using automated tools to scan for vulnerabilities in systems and applications, and conducting manual assessments to identify potential weaknesses that automated tools might miss.

2.4 Enhancing Security Awareness and Training

Ongoing security awareness and training programs are critical for maintaining a security-conscious culture and ensuring that employees are equipped to recognize and respond to threats. Training should be tailored to different roles and skill levels, and should be updated regularly to reflect new threats and best practices.

Example:

- **Phishing Simulations:** Conducting simulated phishing attacks to assess employees' ability to recognize and respond to phishing attempts, and providing targeted training based on the results.

2.5 Leveraging Advanced Technologies

Advanced technologies, such as artificial intelligence (AI) and machine learning (ML), can enhance risk management efforts by providing advanced threat detection, automated responses, and predictive analytics. Leveraging these technologies helps organizations stay ahead of emerging threats and improve their overall security posture.

Example:

- **AI-Driven Threat Detection:** Using AI algorithms to analyze large volumes of data and identify patterns indicative of potential threats, enabling faster and more accurate detection of anomalous activities.

3. Building a Culture of Security

3.1 Promoting Accountability and Ownership

Encouraging accountability and ownership of security practices among employees fosters a culture of security and ensures that individuals understand their role in protecting organizational assets. This includes establishing clear security policies, assigning responsibilities, and holding individuals accountable for adhering to security protocols.

Example:

- **Security Champions:** Designating security champions within different departments to promote security best practices and serve as points of contact for security-related questions or concerns.

3.2 Integrating Security into Business Processes

Integrating security into business processes ensures that security considerations are embedded in all aspects of operations, from system design and development to daily business activities. This holistic approach helps identify and address security risks throughout the lifecycle of business processes.

Example:

- **Secure Development Practices:** Incorporating security practices into the software development lifecycle, such as secure coding standards and regular security testing, to reduce vulnerabilities in applications.

4. Measuring and Reporting on Security Performance

4.1 Defining Key Performance Indicators (KPIs)

Defining and tracking Key Performance Indicators (KPIs) helps measure the effectiveness of security measures and risk management strategies. KPIs should be aligned with organizational goals and provide insights into areas such as incident response times, the number of detected threats, and the effectiveness of security controls.

Example:

- **Incident Response Time:** Measuring the average time taken to detect, contain, and resolve security incidents to evaluate the efficiency of the incident response process.

4.2 Regular Reporting and Review

Regular reporting and review of security performance metrics provide transparency and help identify trends and areas for improvement. Reports should be shared with relevant stakeholders, including senior management, to ensure that security issues are addressed and resources are allocated effectively.

Example:

- **Security Dashboards:** Utilizing dashboards to provide real-time visibility into security metrics, such as threat detection rates and incident response times, and presenting these metrics in regular security reports.

Continuous improvement and the adoption of best practices are essential for effective risk management in cybersecurity. By embracing a proactive approach to enhancing security measures, organizations can address emerging threats, improve their overall security posture, and ensure that their risk management strategies remain relevant and effective. Key practices include establishing a robust risk management framework, implementing layered security controls, conducting regular risk assessments, enhancing security awareness and training, leveraging advanced technologies, and fostering a culture of security. Regular measurement and reporting of security performance metrics further support continuous improvement and help organizations adapt to the evolving threat landscape. Through these efforts, organizations can better protect their assets, maintain business continuity, and respond effectively to security challenges.

4.6 Summary and Key Takeaways

Overview of Risk Management and Incident Response

Effective risk management and incident response are foundational elements of a robust cybersecurity strategy. This chapter has explored the essential components of responding to security incidents, including the formation of an incident response team, defining roles and responsibilities, and implementing a structured response process. It has also highlighted the importance of continuous improvement and best practices in maintaining a strong security posture. By understanding and applying these principles, organizations can enhance their ability to manage risks and respond to incidents more effectively.

Forming and Managing an Incident Response Team

The formation of a dedicated Incident Response Team (IRT) is crucial for managing security incidents efficiently. An effective IRT includes a diverse group of professionals, such as incident response managers, security analysts, IT support, legal representatives, and communication specialists. Each member has specific responsibilities, ranging from overseeing the incident response to analyzing threats and managing communications. Establishing clear roles and responsibilities within the IRT ensures a coordinated and effective response to security incidents.

Incident Response Phases: Preparation to Lessons Learned

The incident response process consists of several critical phases: preparation, detection and identification, containment, eradication, recovery, and lessons learned. Preparation involves setting up the necessary protocols, tools, and training. Detection and identification focus on recognizing and confirming incidents. Containment aims to limit the damage, while eradication addresses the root cause. Recovery involves restoring normal operations, and the lessons learned phase ensures that improvements are made based on the incident review. Each phase plays a vital role in minimizing the impact of security incidents and enhancing future responses.

Continuous Improvement and Best Practices

Continuous improvement is integral to effective risk management. Organizations should regularly review and update their risk management strategies, incorporating feedback from incident post-mortems and risk assessments. Implementing layered security controls, conducting regular risk assessments, and leveraging advanced technologies are key best practices. Additionally, fostering a security-conscious culture through regular training and awareness programs helps maintain an informed and vigilant workforce. By embracing these practices, organizations can adapt to the evolving threat landscape and improve their overall security posture.

Communication and Coordination

Effective communication is essential during a security incident. Internal communication ensures that all relevant stakeholders are informed of the incident status and response actions. External communication manages interactions with customers, partners, regulators, and the media. Clear and consistent messaging helps maintain trust and transparency, while coordination among various teams ensures that response efforts are well-aligned and efficient.

Training and Preparedness

Regular training and preparedness activities, such as tabletop exercises and simulations, are critical for ensuring that the incident response team is well-prepared to handle security incidents. Updating the incident response plan based on training outcomes and evolving threats ensures that the organization remains agile and responsive. Training should be tailored to different roles and skill levels to maximize its effectiveness.

Measuring and Reporting Performance

Defining and tracking Key Performance Indicators (KPIs) helps measure the effectiveness of risk management and incident response efforts. Regular reporting on security performance metrics provides insights into areas of strength and opportunities for improvement. Transparent reporting to senior management and other stakeholders ensures that security issues are addressed promptly and resources are allocated effectively. In summary, a comprehensive approach to risk management and incident response involves forming a well-coordinated incident response team, following a structured response process, and continuously improving security measures. Embracing best practices, effective communication, regular training, and performance measurement are all crucial for enhancing an organization's ability to manage risks and respond to security incidents. By adopting these strategies, organizations can better protect their assets, maintain business continuity, and adapt to the ever-changing cybersecurity landscape.

Chapter 5: Future Trends and Evolving Challenges

5.1 Emerging Threats and Their Impact on Human Factors
5.2 The Role of Artificial Intelligence and Automation in Addressing Human Risks
5.3 Innovations in Security Training and Awareness Programs
5.4 The Importance of Adaptability and Resilience in Security Culture
5.5 Preparing for the Future: Strategies for Long-Term Security Success
5.6 Summary and Key Takeaways

Chapter 5: Future Trends and Evolving Challenges

As cybersecurity evolves, the future presents a mix of opportunities and threats. The integration of artificial intelligence (AI) and machine learning into security infrastructures will significantly shape how organizations detect and respond to emerging risks. AI will enhance automated threat detection, allowing systems to predict and neutralize attacks in real time. However, this very technology also introduces new vulnerabilities, as malicious actors can exploit AI algorithms to develop more sophisticated attacks, including deepfake scams and AI-driven phishing attempts.

One of the critical challenges is the increasing complexity of cyber threats. Advanced persistent threats (APTs) are becoming more difficult to detect as attackers deploy stealth techniques like fileless malware and supply chain compromises. As businesses continue to embrace cloud computing and the Internet of Things (IoT), the attack surface widens, creating additional points of vulnerability. In this environment, traditional perimeter-based security models will no longer suffice; a zero-trust architecture, where every user and device is continuously verified, will become essential.

Another emerging trend is the growing emphasis on data privacy and regulatory compliance. With more stringent laws such as the GDPR and California Consumer Privacy Act, organizations must navigate an evolving legal landscape while securing user data. Failure to comply not only risks penalties but also significant reputational damage.

Finally, the rise of quantum computing, while offering enormous potential in solving complex problems, also threatens to render current encryption methods obsolete. Cybersecurity experts must anticipate and develop quantum-resistant encryption to ensure long-term data security.

In the coming years, organizations must stay agile, investing in cutting-edge technologies while preparing for the ever-changing nature of cyber threats. Those who fail to evolve will face severe consequences.

Introduction

As the cybersecurity landscape continuously evolves, organizations face a myriad of emerging challenges and trends that reshape how they approach risk management and security. The future of cybersecurity is increasingly defined by advancements in technology, shifting threat dynamics, and the evolving nature of digital interactions. One of the most prominent trends is the growing sophistication of cyber threats, driven by advancements in artificial intelligence (AI) and machine learning (ML). Cyber adversaries are leveraging these technologies to create more sophisticated and evasive attack methods, such as AI-driven phishing campaigns and automated malware that can adapt to bypass traditional defenses. This evolution necessitates the development of advanced security measures and adaptive defense mechanisms to counteract increasingly sophisticated threats.

Another significant trend is the expansion of the Internet of Things (IoT) and the subsequent increase in the attack surface for organizations. With the proliferation of IoT devices, from smart home gadgets to industrial control systems, the number of potential entry points for cyberattacks has skyrocketed. Securing these devices presents unique challenges, as they often lack robust security controls and can be difficult to monitor and manage effectively. This trend underscores the importance of implementing comprehensive IoT security strategies, including network segmentation, device authentication, and continuous monitoring.

The rise of remote work and cloud computing has also introduced new challenges and opportunities in cybersecurity. The shift to remote work has expanded the organizational perimeter, making it more difficult to enforce traditional security measures and requiring new approaches to securing remote access. Similarly, the widespread adoption of cloud services necessitates a reevaluation of security practices, including data protection, access controls, and cloud security configurations. Organizations must adapt their strategies to ensure that cloud environments are securely managed and that remote work does not compromise their security posture.

Furthermore, the increasing emphasis on data privacy and regulatory compliance reflects a growing concern for protecting sensitive information and meeting legal obligations. New regulations, such as the General Data Protection Regulation (GDPR) and the California Consumer Privacy Act (CCPA), impose stringent requirements on how organizations handle personal data. Compliance with these regulations is critical, as non-compliance can result in substantial financial penalties and damage to an organization's reputation. This trend highlights the need for robust data governance practices and the integration of privacy considerations into all aspects of cybersecurity.

In conclusion, the future of cybersecurity will be shaped by the convergence of advanced technologies, the expanding attack surface, and evolving regulatory requirements. Organizations must remain vigilant and adaptable, continuously updating their security strategies to address emerging threats and trends. By embracing innovation, adopting proactive security measures, and ensuring compliance with privacy regulations, organizations can navigate the complexities of the cybersecurity landscape and safeguard their digital assets in an increasingly interconnected world.

5.1 Emerging Threats and Their Impact on Human Factors

As the cybersecurity landscape evolves, emerging threats introduce new challenges that significantly impact human factors in security management. The increasing sophistication of cyber threats is not only a technical concern but also a critical factor influencing human behavior, decision-making, and organizational practices. This section explores how emerging threats reshape the human element in cybersecurity, affecting individuals' interactions with security systems and their overall approach to risk management.

1. The Rise of Advanced Persistent Threats (APTs)

Advanced Persistent Threats (APTs) represent a significant evolution in the threat landscape, characterized by highly sophisticated and prolonged cyberattacks aimed at compromising sensitive data and disrupting operations. APTs often employ advanced techniques such as social engineering, spear-phishing, and zero-day vulnerabilities to gain unauthorized access. These threats require a high level of human vigilance and awareness, as attackers often exploit human behavior to infiltrate systems. The impact on human factors is profound, as employees must be trained to recognize and respond to complex phishing attempts and suspicious activities. The psychological pressure and cognitive load associated with detecting and mitigating APTs can lead to increased stress and potential burnout among cybersecurity professionals.

2. The Growing Complexity of Ransomware Attacks

Ransomware attacks have become more sophisticated and disruptive, often involving multiple stages of infection and encryption. Modern ransomware campaigns frequently use advanced evasion techniques, such as polymorphic code and ransomware-as-a-service (RaaS) models, to enhance their effectiveness. The impact on human factors is multifaceted, including increased pressure on IT and security teams to quickly respond to and recover from attacks. Additionally, organizations must address the human element in their preparedness and response strategies, ensuring that employees understand the importance of regular backups, secure data handling practices, and immediate reporting of suspicious activity. The financial and reputational consequences of ransomware attacks also underscore the need for robust incident response planning and employee training.

3. The Influence of Artificial Intelligence and Machine Learning

Artificial Intelligence (AI) and Machine Learning (ML) are increasingly employed by both cyber defenders and attackers. While these technologies offer advanced capabilities for threat detection and response, they also introduce new challenges related to human factors. On the defensive side, AI-driven security systems require skilled personnel to interpret and act upon the insights generated, as well as to manage the potential for false positives and algorithmic biases. On the offensive side, attackers using AI and ML can automate and personalize attacks, making them more difficult to detect and counter. The interaction between humans and AI in cybersecurity necessitates ongoing training and adaptation to ensure that human operators can effectively manage and respond to AI-generated alerts and recommendations.

4. The Impact of Cloud Computing and Remote Work

The proliferation of cloud computing and the shift to remote work have transformed the cybersecurity landscape, presenting new human factor challenges. Cloud environments introduce complexities related to data access, sharing, and management, requiring users to adapt to new security practices and tools. Remote work further complicates security management by expanding the attack surface and reducing control over the physical security of endpoints. Employees must be vigilant about securing their home networks, using strong authentication methods, and adhering to remote work security policies. The human element is critical in maintaining security in these new environments, as individuals must navigate a range of security protocols and adapt to evolving threats.

5. The Challenge of Insider Threats

Insider threats, whether malicious or unintentional, remain a significant concern as organizations face emerging threats. Insiders may exploit their access for personal gain or inadvertently contribute to security breaches due to negligence or lack of awareness. The growing complexity of security systems and the increasing volume of sensitive data heighten the risk of insider threats. Addressing these challenges requires a comprehensive approach to human factors, including robust training programs, clear communication of security policies, and effective monitoring and response mechanisms. Organizations must foster a culture of security awareness and vigilance to mitigate the risks associated with insider threats. Emerging threats in cybersecurity significantly impact human factors, influencing how individuals interact with security systems and respond to risks. Advanced Persistent Threats, sophisticated ransomware attacks, the use of AI and ML, the expansion of cloud computing and remote work, and the challenge of insider threats all require a nuanced understanding of human behavior and decision-making. Organizations must invest in comprehensive training, effective communication, and continuous adaptation to address these evolving threats and enhance their overall security posture. By recognizing and addressing the human factors associated with emerging threats, organizations can better protect their assets and navigate the complexities of the modern cybersecurity landscape.

5.2 The Role of Artificial Intelligence and Automation in Addressing Human Risks

Artificial Intelligence (AI) and automation are playing increasingly critical roles in the realm of cybersecurity, offering innovative solutions to mitigate human-related risks and enhance overall security. As the complexity of cyber threats grows and the human factor continues to be a significant source of vulnerabilities, AI and automation provide powerful tools to address these challenges by improving threat detection, response, and risk management. This section explores how AI and automation are reshaping the cybersecurity landscape and their impact on reducing human risks.

1. Enhancing Threat Detection through AI

AI-powered systems offer advanced capabilities for threat detection by analyzing vast amounts of data in real time. Traditional security tools often struggle to keep pace with the speed and sophistication of modern cyber threats. AI algorithms, particularly those based on machine learning (ML) and deep learning, can process and analyze large volumes of data from various sources, including network traffic, user behavior, and system logs. These algorithms identify patterns and anomalies that may indicate potential threats, enabling faster and more accurate detection of malicious activities. For instance, AI-driven threat detection systems can recognize subtle deviations from normal behavior that might be indicative of a cyber attack, such as unusual login attempts or data access patterns, which human analysts might miss. By automating the initial stages of threat detection, AI reduces the cognitive load on security professionals and enhances their ability to focus on more complex tasks.

2. Automating Incident Response

Automation is a key component in improving the efficiency and effectiveness of incident response. Automated incident response systems can swiftly execute predefined actions in response to detected threats, such as isolating affected systems, blocking malicious IP addresses, or applying security patches. This automation not only accelerates the response time but also reduces the risk of human error during high-pressure situations. For example, an automated system might automatically contain a compromised endpoint and initiate a forensic investigation while alerting the incident response team. By streamlining routine and repetitive tasks, automation allows security professionals to focus on strategic decision-making and complex problem-solving. Additionally, automated response systems can ensure that actions are taken consistently and according to best practices, further reducing the risk of oversight and mistakes.

3. Reducing Human Error with AI-Powered Security Tools

Human error is a significant factor contributing to security breaches and vulnerabilities. AI-powered security tools can help mitigate these risks by providing real-time guidance and support to users. For example, AI-based security platforms can offer contextual recommendations on best practices for secure behavior, such as identifying suspicious emails and suggesting appropriate actions. These tools can also provide continuous feedback and training to users, reinforcing secure behaviors and helping to prevent mistakes that could lead to security incidents. Additionally, AI can enhance the usability of security systems by automating complex configuration tasks and ensuring that security settings are properly applied. By reducing the likelihood of human error and providing actionable insights, AI-driven tools contribute to a more secure and resilient cybersecurity posture.

4. Improving User Behavior Analytics

User Behavior Analytics (UBA) is an area where AI plays a pivotal role in understanding and managing human risks. UBA systems use AI algorithms to analyze patterns of user behavior and identify deviations that may indicate potential security threats. For instance, an AI-driven UBA system might detect unusual access patterns, such as an employee accessing sensitive data outside of their normal work hours or from an unfamiliar location. By analyzing historical behavior and contextual factors, AI can help distinguish between legitimate anomalies and potential security incidents. This advanced analysis enhances the ability to detect insider threats and compromised accounts, providing valuable insights that support proactive risk management. AI-driven UBA systems can also help tailor security training and awareness programs based on observed user behavior, addressing specific areas of concern and improving overall security practices.

5. Addressing Ethical and Privacy Considerations

While AI and automation offer significant benefits in managing human risks, they also raise ethical and privacy considerations that must be addressed. The use of AI in cybersecurity involves the collection and analysis of large amounts of data, including personal and sensitive information. Organizations must ensure that AI systems are designed and implemented in compliance with privacy regulations and ethical standards. This includes transparent data handling practices, securing consent for data collection, and implementing safeguards to protect user privacy. Additionally, organizations should regularly review and update AI algorithms to mitigate biases and ensure fair and equitable treatment of all individuals. By addressing these considerations, organizations can harness the benefits of AI and automation while maintaining trust and ensuring responsible use of technology.

AI and automation are transforming the way organizations address human risks in cybersecurity, offering advanced solutions for threat detection, incident response, and risk management. By leveraging AI-driven tools and automated processes, organizations can enhance their ability to detect and respond to threats, reduce human error, and improve overall security posture. However, it is essential to address ethical and privacy considerations to ensure responsible and effective use of these technologies. As the cybersecurity landscape continues to evolve, AI and automation will play increasingly vital roles in managing human risks and safeguarding digital assets.

5.3 Innovations in Security Training and Awareness Programs

As the cybersecurity landscape becomes more complex and threats evolve, the traditional approaches to security training and awareness programs are no longer sufficient. Innovations in these programs are crucial for ensuring that employees and organizations remain resilient against emerging cyber threats. This section explores the latest advancements in security training and awareness, highlighting how these innovations enhance learning outcomes and better prepare individuals to handle the dynamic nature of cybersecurity.

1. Gamification and Interactive Learning

Gamification is revolutionizing security training by making learning more engaging and interactive. By incorporating game-like elements, such as points, badges, and leaderboards, organizations can transform traditional training modules into immersive experiences that capture participants' attention and foster active participation. Interactive simulations and scenario-based exercises allow employees to practice responding to cyber threats in a controlled environment, enhancing their problem-solving skills and decision-making abilities. For instance, simulated phishing exercises can help users recognize and respond to phishing attempts in a realistic setting, reinforcing their ability to identify suspicious emails and avoid potential traps. The use of gamification not only increases engagement but also improves retention and application of security knowledge.

2. Adaptive Learning Technologies

Adaptive learning technologies leverage AI and machine learning to create personalized training experiences tailored to individual learning styles and needs. These systems analyze user performance and progress to deliver customized content and exercises that address specific knowledge gaps and areas for improvement. For example, an adaptive learning platform might adjust the difficulty level of training modules based on a user's responses, ensuring that they receive appropriate challenges and support. This personalized approach helps maximize learning efficiency and effectiveness, enabling users to acquire and retain security knowledge more effectively. By providing targeted feedback and recommendations, adaptive learning technologies contribute to a more impactful and engaging training experience.

3. Virtual Reality (VR) and Augmented Reality (AR) Training

Virtual Reality (VR) and Augmented Reality (AR) technologies are emerging as powerful tools for enhancing security training. VR creates immersive, simulated environments where users can practice responding to various cyber threats and security incidents in a realistic, interactive setting. For example, VR training can simulate a cyberattack on an organization's network, allowing users to navigate and respond to the threat as if it were occurring in real-time. AR, on the other hand, overlays digital information onto the physical world, providing context-specific guidance and support during security-related tasks. These technologies offer experiential learning opportunities that improve users' ability to apply security concepts and procedures in practical scenarios. By providing immersive and hands-on experiences, VR and AR enhance engagement and reinforce critical security skills.

4. Behavioral Analytics and User Feedback

Behavioral analytics and user feedback are increasingly being integrated into security training programs to provide insights into user performance and effectiveness. By analyzing data on user interactions with training materials, organizations can identify patterns and trends that indicate areas of strength and weakness. This data-driven approach enables continuous improvement of training content and delivery methods, ensuring that programs remain relevant and effective. Additionally, incorporating user feedback into the training process allows organizations to address specific concerns and preferences, leading to a more tailored and impactful learning experience. By leveraging behavioral analytics and feedback, organizations can refine their training programs and better meet the needs of their users.

5. Microlearning and On-Demand Resources

Microlearning involves delivering security training content in short, focused segments that are easily consumable and accessible. This approach allows employees to engage with training materials in brief, manageable sessions, which can be particularly effective for reinforcing key concepts and skills. On-demand resources, such as video tutorials, infographics, and interactive modules, provide employees with the flexibility to access training materials at their convenience. Microlearning and on-demand resources cater to diverse learning preferences and schedules, enabling continuous learning and reinforcement of security knowledge. By offering bite-sized training content and flexible access, organizations can enhance the accessibility and effectiveness of their security awareness programs.

6. Integration of Real-World Threat Intelligence

Incorporating real-world threat intelligence into security training programs helps ensure that the content remains relevant and up-to-date with current threat trends. By using information on recent cyberattacks, emerging threats, and attack vectors, organizations can provide employees with practical examples and case studies that reflect the latest threat landscape. This approach enhances the applicability of training materials and helps users understand the real-world implications of security threats. Additionally, integrating threat intelligence into training programs enables employees to stay informed about new risks and adopt proactive measures to protect against them.

Innovations in security training and awareness programs are transforming the way organizations prepare their employees to handle cyber threats. By leveraging gamification, adaptive learning technologies, VR and AR, behavioral analytics, microlearning, and real-world threat intelligence, organizations can create more engaging, personalized, and effective training experiences. These advancements not only enhance the learning process but also contribute to a more informed and vigilant workforce, better equipped to address the evolving challenges of the cybersecurity landscape. As threats continue to advance, ongoing innovation in training and awareness programs will be crucial for maintaining robust security practices and safeguarding organizational assets.

5.4 The Importance of Adaptability and Resilience in Security Culture

Adaptability and resilience are fundamental attributes for maintaining an effective security culture in the face of an ever-evolving threat landscape. As cyber threats become increasingly sophisticated and the pace of technological change accelerates, organizations must cultivate a security culture that is both flexible and robust. This section delves into the critical importance of adaptability and resilience in security culture and how they contribute to an organization's ability to withstand and recover from cyber incidents.

1. Embracing Change and Innovation

In the dynamic field of cybersecurity, the ability to adapt to new technologies, emerging threats, and shifting regulatory requirements is essential. Organizations must foster a culture that embraces change rather than resists it. This means staying abreast of the latest security trends, technological advancements, and best practices. A security-aware culture encourages continuous learning and innovation, allowing organizations to integrate new tools and methodologies effectively. For example, as organizations adopt cloud computing and mobile technologies, they must adapt their security strategies to address the unique challenges these technologies present. Embracing change involves not only updating security technologies but also adapting policies, procedures, and training programs to ensure that they remain relevant and effective in a rapidly changing environment.

2. Building Resilience Through Preparedness

Resilience in security culture is characterized by an organization's ability to withstand and recover from cyber incidents. Building resilience involves comprehensive preparedness strategies that encompass risk management, incident response, and business continuity planning. Organizations must develop and regularly update incident response plans that outline clear procedures for addressing various types of cyber threats and breaches. This includes establishing communication protocols, defining roles and responsibilities, and conducting regular drills and simulations. Resilient organizations are also equipped with robust backup and recovery systems to ensure data integrity and availability in the event of a cyberattack. By proactively preparing for potential incidents, organizations can minimize the impact of cyber threats and ensure a swift recovery.

3. Cultivating a Culture of Continuous Improvement

A resilient security culture is rooted in the principle of continuous improvement. Organizations should foster an environment where feedback and lessons learned from security incidents are used to refine and enhance security practices. This involves conducting post-incident reviews and analyses to identify weaknesses and areas for improvement. Continuous improvement also requires regular training and awareness programs that evolve based on new threat intelligence and emerging risks. By adopting a proactive approach to security and incorporating feedback into ongoing practices, organizations can strengthen their defenses and better prepare for future challenges.

4. Encouraging Flexibility in Security Practices

Flexibility in security practices is crucial for adapting to evolving threats and changing business needs. Organizations must be willing to adjust their security strategies and protocols as new information becomes available and as their operational environment shifts. For example, changes in organizational structure, such as mergers or expansions, may necessitate updates to security policies and procedures to address new risks and vulnerabilities. Flexibility also involves being open to adopting new technologies and approaches that enhance security effectiveness. By maintaining a flexible approach, organizations can more effectively respond to emerging threats and ensure that their security measures remain aligned with their objectives and risk profile.

5. Promoting a Resilient Mindset Across the Organization

Building a resilient security culture involves instilling a mindset of resilience throughout the organization. This includes fostering a sense of shared responsibility for security among all employees, from executives to front-line staff. A resilient mindset encourages individuals to be proactive in identifying and reporting potential security issues, to stay informed about security best practices, and to participate actively in training and awareness programs. Leadership plays a key role in promoting this mindset by setting an example, reinforcing the importance of security, and providing the necessary resources and support for security initiatives. By cultivating a culture where resilience is valued and practiced, organizations can enhance their overall security posture and better navigate the complexities of the modern threat landscape.

Adaptability and resilience are integral components of a robust security culture. Organizations must embrace change, build resilience through preparedness, cultivate a culture of continuous improvement, encourage flexibility in security practices, and promote a resilient mindset across all levels. By prioritizing these attributes, organizations can effectively manage the evolving challenges of cybersecurity and ensure that their security culture remains strong and capable of withstanding and recovering from cyber threats. In an increasingly dynamic and complex threat environment, the ability to adapt and be resilient is essential for safeguarding organizational assets and maintaining a secure operational environment.

5.5 Preparing for the Future: Strategies for Long-Term Security Success

As the cybersecurity landscape continues to evolve, preparing for the future involves adopting proactive strategies that ensure long-term security success. The dynamic nature of cyber threats, combined with rapid technological advancements, requires organizations to be forward-thinking and adaptive in their approach to security. Implementing strategies for long-term security success involves not only addressing current vulnerabilities but also anticipating future challenges and preparing to meet them effectively.

1. Developing a Forward-Looking Security Strategy

A key aspect of long-term security success is the development of a forward-looking security strategy that aligns with the organization's overall business objectives and risk profile. This strategy should incorporate an understanding of emerging threats, technological trends, and regulatory changes. By staying informed about the latest developments in cybersecurity, organizations can anticipate potential risks and adjust their security measures accordingly. A forward-looking strategy also involves setting clear, measurable security goals and benchmarks, enabling organizations to track progress and make data-driven decisions. Regularly reviewing and updating the security strategy ensures that it remains relevant and effective in addressing evolving threats.

2. Investing in Advanced Technologies and Innovations

Investing in advanced technologies and innovations is crucial for staying ahead of emerging cyber threats. Technologies such as Artificial Intelligence (AI), Machine

Learning (ML), and automation play a significant role in enhancing threat detection, response, and overall security posture. Organizations should explore and adopt cutting-edge solutions that offer advanced capabilities for threat analysis, behavioral monitoring, and incident response. Additionally, investing in research and development can provide insights into new security technologies and methodologies, helping organizations stay at the forefront of cybersecurity advancements. By embracing innovation, organizations can enhance their ability to detect and mitigate threats more effectively.

3. Building and Sustaining a Security-Aware Culture

Long-term security success is heavily influenced by the strength of the organization's security culture. Building and sustaining a security-aware culture involves ongoing efforts to educate and engage employees at all levels. This includes implementing comprehensive training programs, conducting regular security awareness campaigns, and fostering a culture of shared responsibility for security. Leadership plays a crucial role in reinforcing the importance of security and setting the tone for a culture of vigilance and proactive risk management. By creating an environment where security is embedded in daily practices and decision-making, organizations can ensure that employees are well-prepared to handle emerging threats.

4. Enhancing Incident Response and Recovery Capabilities

Effective incident response and recovery capabilities are essential for long-term security success. Organizations should develop and regularly test incident response plans that outline clear procedures for addressing various types of cyber incidents. This includes establishing communication protocols, defining roles and responsibilities, and conducting simulations and drills to test response readiness. Additionally, organizations should invest in robust backup and recovery solutions to ensure data integrity and availability in the event of a cyberattack. Enhancing incident response and recovery capabilities helps organizations minimize the impact of security incidents and ensures a swift and efficient recovery.

5. Fostering Collaboration and Information Sharing

Collaboration and information sharing are vital for staying ahead of cyber threats and achieving long-term security success. Organizations should actively participate in industry groups, threat intelligence communities, and information sharing platforms to exchange insights and best practices. By collaborating with peers, partners, and cybersecurity experts, organizations can gain valuable insights into emerging threats, vulnerabilities, and effective mitigation strategies. Information sharing also enables organizations to contribute to the collective defense against cyber threats, enhancing the overall security posture of the industry and community.

6. Planning for Regulatory and Compliance Changes

As cybersecurity regulations and compliance requirements continue to evolve, organizations must proactively plan for and adapt to these changes. Staying informed about relevant regulations, standards, and industry requirements is essential for ensuring ongoing compliance and avoiding potential legal and financial penalties. Organizations should regularly review and update their security policies and procedures to align with regulatory changes and industry best practices. By integrating compliance considerations into the security strategy, organizations can mitigate risks and ensure that their security practices meet legal and regulatory expectations. Preparing for the future and achieving long-term security success requires a multifaceted approach that includes developing a forward-looking security strategy, investing in advanced technologies, building a security-aware culture, enhancing incident response and recovery capabilities, fostering collaboration, and planning for regulatory changes. By adopting these strategies, organizations can effectively navigate the evolving cybersecurity landscape and ensure their security measures remain robust and resilient. As threats continue to advance and technology evolves, a proactive and strategic approach to security will be essential for safeguarding organizational assets and achieving long-term success in the realm of cybersecurity.

5.6 Summary and Key Takeaways

In this chapter, we have explored critical aspects of preparing for future security challenges and ensuring long-term success in cybersecurity. The dynamic nature of the cyber threat landscape necessitates a proactive and adaptive approach, emphasizing the importance of strategic planning, technological investment, cultural development, and collaborative efforts. Understanding these elements is crucial for organizations seeking to enhance their security posture and maintain resilience against evolving threats.

1. The Imperative of a Forward-Looking Security Strategy

Developing a forward-looking security strategy is foundational to long-term success. This strategy must anticipate emerging threats, technological trends, and regulatory changes. By aligning security goals with business objectives and continuously updating the strategy in response to new information, organizations can better prepare for potential risks. The emphasis on foresight and strategic alignment ensures that security measures remain effective and relevant, addressing both current and future challenges.

2. Investing in Technological Advancements

The role of advanced technologies in cybersecurity cannot be overstated. Investments in AI, machine learning, and automation are pivotal for enhancing threat detection, response, and overall security efficacy. These technologies provide advanced capabilities for analyzing vast amounts of data, identifying patterns, and automating responses to threats. Organizations that prioritize technological innovation position themselves advantageously in the fight against cyber threats, leveraging cutting-edge solutions to stay ahead of adversaries.

3. Cultivating a Security-Aware Culture

A robust security culture is integral to long-term security success. Building and maintaining a culture of security awareness involves continuous education, training, and engagement of employees. Leadership plays a critical role in reinforcing the importance of security and embedding it into organizational practices. By fostering a culture where security is a shared responsibility and integral to daily operations, organizations can enhance their overall resilience and preparedness.

4. Strengthening Incident Response and Recovery

Effective incident response and recovery capabilities are essential for minimizing the impact of cyber incidents and ensuring swift recovery. Developing comprehensive incident response plans, conducting regular drills, and investing in backup and recovery solutions are key strategies for enhancing these capabilities. By preparing for potential incidents and having robust recovery mechanisms in place, organizations can mitigate damage and resume normal operations more efficiently.

5. Embracing Collaboration and Information Sharing

Collaboration and information sharing are critical for staying ahead of cyber threats and achieving security success. Participation in industry groups, threat intelligence communities, and information sharing platforms enhances collective defense and provides valuable insights into emerging threats and effective countermeasures. By working together with peers and cybersecurity experts, organizations can strengthen their own security posture and contribute to broader industry resilience.

6. Planning for Regulatory and Compliance Changes

Proactively addressing regulatory and compliance changes is crucial for maintaining ongoing security and avoiding potential penalties. Staying informed about relevant regulations and integrating compliance considerations into security practices ensures that organizations meet legal requirements and industry standards. Regularly updating policies and procedures to reflect regulatory changes helps organizations manage risks and maintain compliance effectively. In summary, preparing for the future of cybersecurity involves a comprehensive approach that includes strategic planning, technological investment, cultural development, enhanced incident response, collaboration, and regulatory compliance. By focusing on these key areas, organizations can build a resilient and adaptive security framework capable of addressing both current and emerging challenges. The insights and strategies discussed in this chapter provide a roadmap for achieving long-term security success, ensuring that organizations remain vigilant and prepared in an ever-evolving cyber landscape.

www.ingramcontent.com/pod-product-compliance
Lightning Source LLC
Chambersburg PA
CBHW052350220526
45465CB00003BA/1045